KATIE WHITE

STUDENT
SELF-ASSESSMENT

Data Notebooks, Portfolios,
& Other Tools to Advance Learning

Solution Tree | Press

Copyright © 2022 by Solution Tree Press

Materials appearing here are copyrighted. With one exception, all rights are reserved. Readers may reproduce only those pages marked "Reproducible." Otherwise, no part of this book may be reproduced or transmitted in any form or by any means (electronic, photocopying, recording, or otherwise) without prior written permission of the publisher.

555 North Morton Street
Bloomington, IN 47404
800.733.6786 (toll free) / 812.336.7700
FAX: 812.336.7790

email: info@SolutionTree.com
SolutionTree.com

Visit **go.SolutionTree.com/assessment** to download the free reproducibles in this book.

Printed in the United States of America

Library of Congress Cataloging-in-Publication Data

Names: White, Katie, 1977- author.
Title: Student self-assessment : data notebooks, portfolios, and other
   tools to advance learning / Katie White.
Description: Bloomington, IN : Solution Tree Press, [2022] | Includes
   bibliographical references and index.
Identifiers: LCCN 2021039559 (print) | LCCN 2021039560 (ebook) | ISBN
   9781952812859 (paperback) | ISBN 9781952812866 (ebook)
Subjects: LCSH: Students--Self-rating of. | Portfolios in education. |
   Teaching--Aids and devices.
Classification: LCC LB3051 .W48846 2022 (print) | LCC LB3051 (ebook) |
   DDC 371.26--dc23
LC record available at https://lccn.loc.gov/2021039559
LC ebook record available at https://lccn.loc.gov/2021039560

Solution Tree
Jeffrey C. Jones, CEO
Edmund M. Ackerman, President

Solution Tree Press
President and Publisher: Douglas M. Rife
Associate Publisher: Sarah Payne-Mills
Art Director: Rian Anderson
Managing Production Editor: Kendra Slayton
Editorial Director: Todd Brakke
Copy Chief: Jessi Finn
Senior Production Editor: Christine Hood
Content Development Specialist: Amy Rubenstein
Proofreader: Mark Hain
Text and Cover Designer: Abigail Bowen
Editorial Assistants: Sarah Ludwig and Elijah Oates

ACKNOWLEDGMENTS

I would like to acknowledge that this book was written on Treaty 6 territory. As a Canadian and as part of my commitment to truth and reconciliation, I would like to express my gratitude for the treaties, which have allowed me to live and work as a guest on this land. Treaty 6 territory is the traditional homeland of indigenous peoples of Saskatchewan, past and present.

Thank you to Cassie, Nicole, and Tom, who invited me to explore assessment in new and rich ways. What a journey and a privilege!

Thank you to Rodney, who patiently shared days with this book on not one, but two summer camping trips. Your unconditional support is a true gift.

Solution Tree Press would like to thank the following reviewers:

Tonya Alexander
English Teacher (NBCT)
Owego Free Academy
Owego, New York

Charles Ames Fischer
Educational Consultant
Decatur, Tennessee

Justin Schafer
Teacher on Special Assignment
Benton Elementary School
Goshen, Indiana

Jennifer Steele
Assistant Principal
Northside High School
Fort Smith, Arkansas

TABLE OF CONTENTS

Reproducible pages are in italics.

About the Author..ix

INTRODUCTION
Embracing Student Self-Assessment..................... 1
    Examples of Student Self-Assessment........................... 2
    Data Notebooks and Portfolios for Self-Assessment................ 5
    About This Book... 6
    Conclusion... 7

CHAPTER 1
Making a Compelling Case for Self-Assessment.......... 9
    Three Paradigm Shifts.. 10
    The Purpose of Data Notebooks and Portfolios................... 15
    Other Self-Assessment Tools.................................. 16
    Where to Start... 17
    Questions to Guide Conversation and Reflection.................. 17

CHAPTER 2
Setting Up a Self-Assessment Process and
Documenting Learning................................19
    Considerations for Self-Assessment............................ 20
    How to Make This Work 24
    Where to Start... 34
    Tools to Support Self-Assessment.............................. 34
    Questions to Guide Conversation and Reflection.................. 35
    All About Me: Early Elementary................................ 36

All About Me 37
What Would You Like to Do? 38
My Dreams and Ambitions 39
My Learning Story Sample: Early Elementary 40
My Learning Story Sample 41
Sample Unit Tracker 42
Monitoring My Learning 43
Documenting and Reflecting on My Learning 44

CHAPTER 3
Engaging in Analysis and Reflection 45

Considerations for Self-Assessment 48
How to Make This Work 50
Where to Start 60
Tools to Support Self-Assessment 60
Questions to Guide Conversation and Reflection 61
Margin Symbols 62
Reflection on a Work Sample: Single-Point Rubric 63
Tracking My Progress 64
Growth Card 65
Reflecting on Success Criteria 66
Most Important Things 67
My Action Plan 68
Assess and Reflect on Reading Skills 69

CHAPTER 4
Imagining Possibilities and Setting Goals 71

Elements of Goal Setting 73
Considerations for Self-Assessment 75
How to Make This Work 80
Where to Start 81
Tools to Support Self-Assessment 81
Questions to Guide Conversation and Reflection 82
Reflecting on Competencies 84
Today's Goal 85
Short- and Long-Term Goals 86

Reflecting and Goal Setting: English Language Arts 87
Connecting Long-Term Goals to Short-Term Targets 88
My Goals 89
Goal Setting During Exploration 90
Daily Goal Setting 91
Reflecting and Goal Setting Prior to Sharing Learning With Others 92
Daily Decision Making 93
Reaching My Goal 94
My Assessment Record 95
It's All Down to Decisions: Monitoring Goals 96

CHAPTER 5
Celebrating Growth 97
Considerations for Self-Assessment. 99
How to Make This Work 101
Where to Start 101
Tools to Support Self-Assessment 102
Questions to Guide Conversation and Reflection. 102
I Can Self-Assess! 104
Celebrations With Others 105
How I Would Like to Celebrate 106
Celebration Time!. 107

CHAPTER 6
Examining Age, Security, Families, and Other Factors 109
Self-Assessment and Students in Early Elementary Classrooms. 109
Safety and Privacy 111
Family Engagement 113
Teacher and Student Roles 113
How to Overcome Common Barriers 116
Where to Start 118
Questions to Guide Conversation and Reflection. 118

Epilogue 121

APPENDIX
Example Self-Assessment Sequence....................123
    Getting Ready to Write.................................125
    Writing Sample: *Life Is an Elevator*..........................126
    Single-Point Rubric for "Life as a Metaphor"....................127
    Data Collection: Transition Words and Use of Examples............128
    Analysis and Reflection................................129
    Writing Sample Revision: *Life Is an Elevator*....................130
    Final Reflection......................................131
    My Goals and Celebration..............................132

References and Resources..........................133

Index..137

ABOUT THE AUTHOR

 **KATIE WHITE** is coordinator of learning for the North East School Division in Saskatchewan, Canada, and an educational consultant. With more than twenty-five years working in education, she has been a district and in-school administrator, learning coach, and K–12 classroom teacher.

Katie spends her days working to transform the educational experience for teachers and students. She has been an integral part of her school division's multiyear journey through educational reform, including a response to new curricula that resulted in a standards or outcome-based approach to assessment, learning, and reporting. Katie has a passion for helping educators develop a personalized understanding of the connections between curriculum, assessment, and instruction, and creative approaches for reaching and teaching every learner in every classroom.

In living out this passion, Katie not only works within her system but serves as an independent educational consultant, speaking with and facilitating teacher and administrator groups worldwide. Her sense of humor and flexible and responsive approaches to adult learning make her a sought-after professional support for systems and schools. She is a co-moderator of the well-known All Things Assessment (#ATAssessment) Twitter chat and a frequent contributor to the All Things Assessment blog (http://allthingsassessment.info/blog), and serves as the president of the nonprofit Canadian Assessment for Learning Network.

In addition to *Student Self-Assessment*, she has authored *Softening the Edges: Assessment Practices That Honor K–12 Teachers and Learners* and *Unlocked: Assessment as the Key to Unlocking Everyday Creativity in the Classroom*.

Katie received a bachelor of education and master of education in curriculum studies from the University of Saskatchewan.

To learn more about Katie's work, visit www.kwhiteconsulting.com, or follow her @KatieWhite426 on Twitter.

To book Katie White for professional development, contact pd@SolutionTree.com.

INTRODUCTION

Embracing Student Self-Assessment

I have an unwavering belief in the abilities and potential of learners, young and old. This is an important place to start a book on student self-assessment, because this type of assessment depends on the skills and strengths of those who engage in it. I also possess an unfailing optimism that students can learn and grow; that with guidance and support, students can make decisions and engage in actions that will result in increased skills, richer understanding, and higher levels of engagement, independence, and efficacy. As I see it, ability, potential, and optimism are foundational to the business of education, and learning how to nurture these attributes in each and every learner our systems serve makes sense. Indeed, I suspect educators would agree that the activities and experiences to which teachers and students devote their days must certainly lead to growth, in both the short and long term.

Self-assessment, as a way to build potential, ability, and optimism, has preoccupied me for quite some time. It began with my work in the area of arts education, which had a strong influence on my recognizing its importance. The necessity for artists of all ages to direct their own decisions about their creative work has been foundational to my pedagogy. My interest in self-assessment intensified when my home province renewed its English language arts learning outcomes, and self-assessment became a key focus for specific learning goals. I became increasingly committed to learning how to develop strong self-assessment skills in learners as I spent time building tools and supports and working alongside teachers within classroom contexts. Adding to this interest has been an increasing recognition of the importance of intentional conversations between teachers and students as a way of drawing students into reflection and decision making. All these catalysts pointed to a need to explore this topic further.

As I began to learn more, one of the first things I acknowledged was that self-assessment was occurring more often in my classroom than I originally thought. Indeed, when students approached me expressing disappointment in their work, they were engaging in a simple form of self-assessment. They recognized that their efforts (current state; often expressed through phrases like "This sucks!" and "I hate doing this!") had not yet yielded desired results (future state reflected in personal goals). By knowing this, learners took an important first step in comparing their current products (such as assignments, essays, artworks, journal entries), performances (such as presentations, dramatic works, games), and processes (such as constructing an argument, building a model) to a future goal. If I could leverage these moments and work with students to design action steps, together, we might be able to advance learning at an accelerated rate.

In the introduction, you will learn why embracing self-assessment is such an important part of student learning and growth. I begin by providing some examples of student self-assessment to show how you can implement it across grade levels. You will then explore the idea of data notebooks and portfolios as a means for students to document, organize, and record their work for reflection and self-assessment. Finally, I provide a chapter-by-chapter overview of the book, giving insight into the topics supporting a successful process for student self-reflection in your classroom.

Examples of Student Self-Assessment

Once I developed a personal commitment to exploring and enhancing self-assessment as part of an enriched learning process, I began to look for and facilitate examples of self-assessment in both my own teaching contexts and in those of colleagues with whom I was working. I wanted to see where it might naturally occur and whether students of all ages could engage in reflection, goal setting, and decision making. I was excited to discover that it could exist in all K–12 classrooms, in several different formats, and at varied times within the learning process.

In this book, I discuss self-assessment in early learning classrooms (preK–3), elementary and middle school classrooms (grades 4–8), and high school classrooms (grades 9–12). Some self-assessment processes can be successful across all grade levels, while others require developmentally appropriate skills. Adapting the strategies in this book through the lens of *How might this work for my students?* is a great approach. I have tried to support this question by adding suggested grade bands to the resources.

The following scenarios are a few examples of self-assessment that I either facilitated myself or observed other teachers facilitate within various classroom contexts. Student and teacher names and descriptions have been changed to protect their anonymity. These moments occurred during independent self-assessment sessions, group reflections about first and second versions of products, emergent conversations while engaged in creative play, and formal conferences with artifacts to support the discussion. By sharing these examples, I hope to demonstrate the variety of ways self-assessment and reflection can occur in classrooms across grade levels and subject areas.

KINDERGARTEN CLASSROOM

The teacher crouches down beside the two young students on the floor. One is lying on his stomach, holding his head up with his hands as he gazes at the scene before him. The second is sitting on her knees, leaning in and placing another dinosaur among the wooden blocks.

"What are you working on?" the teacher gently asks, trying not to interrupt their flow with her question.

"I am putting this T-rex in the city," the second student explains. "He is going to knock some buildings down pretty soon."

"Yeah," her classmate confirms. "We are getting ready for a big crash." It is clear the two learners have a plan together.

"How will you know it is time to make that happen?" the teacher asks.

"When we have it all set up," the kneeling student explains. "We have to have everything ready before we do it. We are both trying to get all the stuff set up together."

"What needs to be ready?" the teacher probes further. "What else do you need to do? What is your plan?"

"We have to put the cars in there." The student gestures beside her, so the teacher can see a pile of cars waiting to be positioned. "They are going to be part of the crash," she patiently explains.

"How will you know when it is time?" the teacher asks again.

"When we get all the stuff in there. The T-rex needs lots of stuff to knock down."

"Who will be making things crash? Who will hold the T-rex?" the teacher wonders.

The two students pause and look at each other. They hadn't gotten that far.

"We will take turns," one student declares. The second student nods her head in agreement. "Yeah, Billy first and then me. He is going to save some stuff for me to knock down. That's the best part."

"How will you make sure blocks don't go flying and hurt another student?" the teacher asks, unable to resist inviting a safety conversation.

"We will be careful," they assert. "We won't crash it too big. We will tell everyone to move back when we are ready."

"Sounds like you have a plan. I will check back to hear how it went." The teacher stands up and leaves the students to their thinking.

SIXTH-GRADE CLASSROOM

"Okay," the teacher begins, "let's gather around our paintings and talk about what we notice. Think about the decisions you made with your first try and which decisions you changed in your second attempt."

The teacher can see students looking at the two versions of their own landscapes, even though everyone's work is on the table. It is natural to want to focus on their own efforts.

The teacher extends an invitation, "Who is willing to take a risk and be the first person to reflect?"

One learner raises her hand. "I will try," she offers. "I like the colors in my first one, but I didn't like how dark the sky was. I wanted it to be like the one you showed us, but I put too much paint in the water. Then, when I tried to fix it, I rubbed a bit of a hole in my paper." She leans forward and taps her paper in the spot where it has worn thin from scrubbing. "In my second one," she continues, "I asked you for help before, and then I tested my color on a different piece of paper before putting it on my picture." She pauses and looks at her second landscape.

"How do you feel about your second attempt?" the teacher asks. "Did you like this color better?"

"Kind of," she begins. "I wish I could make a color that was halfway between the two. I think this one is too light when it is on my whole sky."

"Do you want to try this a third time?" the teacher asks.

"Yeah, I think I do. I also want to add more trees."

EIGHTH-GRADE CLASSROOM

"Before we begin, I would like you to find the data you converted into a bar graph in your data notebooks at the end of the day yesterday." The teacher gestures to the bar graph example they had created together as a class after students completed a formative assessment and worked in pairs to check their responses. "We are going to spend a few minutes reflecting on our strengths and choosing a goal that will guide our learning and practice today."

The teacher pauses and lets students locate their data notebooks in their desks. "If you are having trouble finding the graph, remember to look in your science section," he reminds them.

"Is this the one?" A student holds up the notebook, clearly on the correct page.

"Look at our example up here," the teacher taps on the chart paper. "If your graph looks like this one and it shows your results from yesterday's formative assessment, then you are on the right page."

The teacher silently takes comfort in holding this student accountable for deciding whether the data set was the correct one; it is hard and intentional work to resist verifying whether a decision was a good one, and students often test his resolve. "Don't work harder than your students," he whispers to himself.

The teacher turns back to the class, "Once you find your graph, please answer the questions I have on the whiteboard. Record your reflections right underneath the graph." He gestures to the questions. "Please note that each question invites you to explain the reasons for your answers. Your reasons should be clear both in your graph and within yesterday's formative assessment."

Two questions on the whiteboard read:
1. What skills went well on this formative assessment? How do you know? Be sure to provide specific evidence from your graph and your assessment.
2. What skill will you focus on strengthening today? Why did you choose this skill? Be sure to provide specific evidence from your graph and your assessment.

The students are used to these kinds of questions, and they begin to reflect, referring to both their graphs and the formative assessment that sits in front of the graph in their notebooks.

"Great," the teacher affirms. "Remember to make a note of your goal and the strategies you are going to try on your goal sheet, and we will check in at the end of class."

TENTH-GRADE CLASSROOM

"Davis, can I chat with you about your reflection before you start your next assignment?" The teacher holds up the reflection form and accompanying Giving Effective Feedback assignment. Davis nods, walks back to the teacher's table, and sits down beside her. She arranges the criteria-focused reflection form and Davis's written feedback side by side so they can both see them easily.

The teacher begins by pointing to a comment next to the second criterion on the form. "You reflected that you didn't provide a specific example to support your feedback suggestion to the author of the writing sample you looked at. I read your feedback, and I agree that an example might have helped clarify your suggestion that the author add clearer transitions. This was an accurate reflection." She pauses a moment and looks at Davis to determine whether her observations are making sense. Davis nods, and she continues, "Examples can really help a writer imagine new ways for constructing their writing."

"I like examples when people are giving me feedback," Davis confirms. "It helps me see how I could change things to make them better. But what if I don't like their example? Do I have to do it?"

"No. That is the beauty of feedback," the teacher explains. "It is supposed to cause us to think, but it isn't a recipe to follow. We have to figure out what to do on our own. That is why your reflection makes sense—an example or two might have helped the writer think more clearly about how they could solve the challenge you identified."

"I get it," Davis replies. "I should have done that. I knew it."

"Right. However, you noticed this before you handed in your feedback to me and also returned it to the author. I was wondering why, if you knew you needed an example, you didn't just add it to your feedback?" This puzzles the teacher. If Davis knows better, why doesn't he apply the self-assessment to the assignment?

"I thought I couldn't," Davis explains. "I thought this reflection was a different assignment."

The teacher nods her head, suddenly understanding what is going on. She realizes that Davis saw the feedback and the accompanying reflection as two different assignments rather than connected. She follows up by asking, "Now that we have talked, can you imagine a way to enhance your feedback? Do you have any changes you'd like to make so the author feels supported and clear about your suggestions?"

"Yes, I'd like to add some examples to my comments so I'm clearer. I need to help the author think, right? I want to try that. Maybe I will ask a couple of extra questions, too."

Self-assessment can occur in different ways and with different areas of focus. However, there are some common attributes present that establish these scenarios as representative of assessment in general and self-assessment in particular. The act of assessing anything requires a comparison of the skills and understanding indicated by evidence *in this moment* to desired skills and understanding as represented within goals (in education, this most often means standards, outcomes, or competencies). Assessment becomes *self*-assessment when learners play an active role in gathering and analyzing evidence, setting short-term goals, making decisions to advance those goals, and reflecting on the success of those decisions. The specific attributes that help shift our assessment focus to self-assessment are as follows.

- **Attention:** The teacher draws students' attention to their *current state* (the most recent evidence of the state of developing skills and understanding), which may include describing a product or performance as well as processes or decisions that are occurring.

- **Focus:** A goal, desired outcome, or *future state* receives the focus. This future state may involve longer-term standards, outcomes, or competencies. Teachers might drive these standards or goals, or students might determine shorter-term actions or decisions.

- **Evidence:** There is an emphasis on evidence that supports the description of current state, the assertion of the goal, or both. In the case of self-assessment, students are highly involved in the collection and analysis of evidence.

- **Effort:** The teacher, mentor, or facilitator makes efforts to establish actions, decisions,

strategies, or steps the learner might take moving forward.
- **Time:** The teacher, mentor, or facilitator sets aside time to focus on both strengths and needs or areas for growth.
- **Investment and ownership:** The student shows evidence of investment and ownership over decision making.
- **Support:** The teacher, mentor, or facilitator supports the students in making decisions and establishing and then working toward goals. In other words, self-assessment still requires teacher guidance.

Understanding these important indicators of self-assessment can help teachers (or mentors and facilitators) advance students' self-assessment skills in daily moments of teaching and learning. In this book, I expand on each of these critical aspects of self-assessment and offer structures, templates, and tools to facilitate a variety of self-assessment processes. I specifically investigate data notebooks and portfolios, including how to engage students of all ages in quantitative and qualitative analysis. This book also discusses methods for students to set goals and strategies to encourage reflection, feedback, and celebration. By the end, I hope you understand the promise of self-assessment, the ways you might develop this complex skill in learners, and how to embed it in the daily lived experiences of individual classroom and school spaces.

Data Notebooks and Portfolios for Self-Assessment

In this book, I devote a good amount of time to data notebooks and portfolios—two tools for documenting learning and engaging in and organizing self-assessment. This is the case for a number of reasons. First, many school systems have already attempted to utilize data notebooks or portfolios as part of their approach to improving learner outcomes, and so they are familiar to educators. Second, data sets (for example, data related to benchmark assessments, data reflecting degrees of proficiency in relation to learning goals, or perceptual data reflecting parent and student engagement) and assessment artifacts (for example, writing samples and rubrics, assignments, tests, and photo and video samples) are readily available to teachers and students. Because they are already part of the educational landscape, it makes sense to figure out how to use learning data and artifacts to engage learners and enhance learning outcomes. Third, data notebooks and portfolios are highly adaptable and flexible ways to collect and organize information important to learning. Teachers and students can use them often and in many ways.

With both data notebooks and portfolios, assessment becomes more intentional, robust, and conducive to student reflection and goal setting. The data and artifacts collected over time provide a window into how learning develops in the short term and how this short-term progress contributes to continual growth. It allows students and teachers to connect discrete assignments and tasks to broader educational goals, and it makes visible the relationships between day-to-day operations and the skills and understanding that have deeply significant meaning to students. By documenting evidence within a portfolio or data notebook, teachers can draw attention to decision making and highlight strategies and dispositions that lead to successful learning in a wide variety of contexts and across curricular boundaries.

How educators choose to invite students to reflect on and analyze their own work can vary. And how teachers connect with families and share growth and progress can be individualized by either the teacher or student. But by collecting multiple data samples and artifacts of learning in a single place, like within a data notebook or portfolio, teachers can facilitate connections and relationships between learning goals, topics, and texts that surpass what is possible when teachers and students examine and reflect on assignments or lessons in isolation. Portfolios and data notebooks are about examining longitudinal growth in relation to big questions and deeply meaningful goals.

When you consider or extend the idea of data notebooks and portfolios, think about what works best in your classroom and what materials and technology you have available. Students can draw self-assessment tools, artifacts, data samples, graphs, and goal sheets on graph paper or write them out on loose-leaf paper and glue them into notebooks. Students also can place them in physical folders and organize them by theme or chronology. Another possibility is to collect and organize digital files on a computer, a tablet, or an online platform. The options are endless, and the format must be as accessible as possible. Use the best format for the specific students in your classroom based on what is easily accessible. Talk with colleagues and learn what has worked for them. Through social media, explore the practices of teaching colleagues. Choose the format that works best for you, your students, and their families. For example, consider access to technology within your classroom and in family homes before diving into digital formats.

In the end, the tool must serve the users. Start small and dream big. Data notebooks and portfolios can change how students think about their learning and their role within the classroom. You can use them to share with families how your school develops learning. This is the kind of powerful paradigm shift that can change learning outcomes for students. As you read, continue to ask yourself, "How might this work in my classroom and school?"

About This Book

Each chapter in this book explores an important component of self-assessment. By the end, you will have a clear sense of how to navigate self-assessment and learn to leverage it in a variety of ways to advance student learning, confidence, and self-perception. You will explore how to set up, organize, and reinforce data notebooks, portfolios, and other self-assessment tools, and learn ways to help students analyze the information they gather and determine relevant goals and actions that facilitate both short-term progress and long-term growth. You also will learn how to encourage students to celebrate their success and regroup for additional practice and learning when needed. Lastly, you will become clear about the role of both students and teachers in the self-assessment process. Whether you wish to set up data notebooks, portfolios, or simply find a goal-setting process that works, you will access a variety of tools and supports for your specific needs.

For each aspect of self-assessment, I will share background information (who is involved, what actions need to be taken, and when it makes sense to engage in each process) and the rationale (why this aspect of self-assessment is so critical), and offer templates, tools, and additional supports (how to engage in the work) for each component in subsequent chapters.

Following is a chapter overview. Please note that chapters 1 and 6 follow a different structure and serve a different purpose than chapters 2 through 5, which explore specific practical components of self-assessment. The first chapter explores reasons why self-assessment is important to student growth, worthy of time and attention, and a process that supports continual growth. The final chapter discusses the specific nuances of self-assessment that can enhance the process in a variety of contexts and bring families into the process.

Chapters 2 through 5 follow a repeating format to help with implementation. Each chapter begins with a scenario, followed by questions to guide reflection. Next, each offers specific considerations, practical ways to make each component of self-assessment work, and specific tools to support self-assessment in classrooms. This chapter structure provides increasingly specific and tangible ways to engage students in self-assessment, with a focus on providing tools to support this work.

Chapter 1 offers research and rationale for why self-assessment should be an embedded practice within all classrooms, at every grade level. Chapter 2 provides strategies to plan for and prepare students to engage in self-assessment, including documenting learning as it develops, from beginning to end. Chapter 3 offers educators specific and varied ways to engage students in analyzing their own data and assessment artifacts to stimulate decision making. Chapter 4 provides processes, templates, and tools for inviting students to look to the future and set their own goals for growth and learning. Chapter 5 examines the realms of achievement, growth, and acknowledgement and how to select celebration strategies that meet students' needs. Finally, chapter 6 explores aspects of self-assessment (for example, age, security, and families) that require some specific attention for self-assessment to live up to its potential.

At the end of each chapter, you will find a section titled Where to Start, which outlines steps to begin each key process involved in self-assessment. You also will find reflection questions you can use to begin important conversations with colleagues as a catalyst for staff exploration, or simply as a prompt for personal reflection and growth. Use these questions in the way that makes the most sense for you. Chapters 2 through 5 each conclude with several reproducible tools and templates to help you and your students engage with the self-assessment process. Finally, the book concludes with a helpful appendix, which shows an example self-assessment sequence.

If self-assessment is new to you or if you have experienced challenges when attempting various self-assessment processes, you may want to read the book from start to finish. However, you can also search for specific templates or explore specific topics for self-assessment and use them immediately in your classroom. Each educator is in a unique place in their own assessment journey, and this book offers flexible entry points into this very important topic. Perhaps the best way to decide how to use this book is to ask students where they feel they need the most support. Any time teachers invite students to make decisions and offer suggestions, they are honoring student voice as a critical part of self-assessment.

Conclusion

No matter where you are in the journey, the importance of the self-assessment process cannot be denied. Renowned assessment researchers and authors Jan Chappuis, Rick Stiggins, Steve Chappuis, and Judith Arter (2012) remind us:

> Any activity that requires students to reflect on what they are learning and share their progress both reinforces the learning and helps develop insights into themselves as learners. These kinds of activities give students the opportunity to notice their own strengths, to see how far they have come, and to feel in control of the conditions of their success. (p. 34)

With this in mind, start where it makes sense to do so, reflect often, and make changes as needed. As educators, we need the same opportunities as our students to self-assess our own progress and learn from our own mistakes. Good luck and happy reading!

CHAPTER 1

Making a Compelling Case for Self-Assessment

We shape our tools and then our tools shape us.
—*Father John M. Culkin*

Given the sheer number of learning goals every grade level and subject area have to contend with and the reality of time constraints in 21st century classrooms, it is fair to hesitate before adopting any additional instructional or assessment practices. Self-assessment is a complex skill, in and of itself, and it requires instructional time and recursive practice in order to impact learning outcomes. Furthermore, there are levels of nuance in implementing it within daily routines, and so it is fair to ask, "Is self-assessment really worth the time and effort?"

Research clearly establishes the importance of self-assessment for formative or learning purposes (Andrade, 2019; Andrade & Du, 2007; Gregory, Cameron, & Davies, 2011; Hattie, 2012; Organisation for Economic Co-operation and Development [OECD], 2017; Ross, 2006; Sanchez, Atkinson, Koenka, Moshontz, & Cooper, 2017). However, when self-assessment is part of summative decision making, the results are less accurate and, thus, less favorable (Admiraal, Huisman, & Pilli, 2015; Baxter & Norman, 2011). With this discrepancy in mind, this book focuses on the kinds of self-assessment practices that lead to analysis, reflection, and instructional decision making to enhance the quality of products or performances. In this way, investment in self-assessment will have a significant impact on learning.

So, what is self-assessment? Researcher Heidi L. Andrade (2019) defines it this way: "Self-assessment is the act of monitoring one's processes and products in order to make adjustments that deepen learning and enhance performance." It is the act of noticing and remembering personal events, consequences, and actions as related to choices and decisions, and measuring the degree to which they have met a desired result. From effective self-assessment emerge plans for future actions based on goals. In other words, self-assessment means taking stock of where we are, determining where we want to be, and making decisions to address the space between the two.

Despite the potential of self-assessment, practically speaking, it can be challenging to do with students in meaningful and successful ways. There is no doubt that teachers try—they ask students to reflect on a project, or they ask learners to set goals each term—but students might seem uncommitted, goals may seem contrived, and reflections can seem shallow. It can be tough to make self-assessment work in classrooms and have it not feel like it is taking time away from learning. It is understandable that teachers might abandon it in favor of strategies and approaches that feel more authentic and seem to result in better and faster outcomes.

For self-assessment to be effective, educators need to work out the following aspects of this process.

- *Why* they might do it
- *When* it makes sense to make time for it
- *How* they can make it part of their instructional practice (as opposed to being just "another thing to do")

- *How* it will impact instructional design and assessment systems
- *Who* to involve

Effective self-assessment is more than a simple action—it is a catalyst for something much greater than itself. When self-assessment occurs in authentic and meaningful ways, it contributes to students experiencing not only richer learning but increased efficacy, decision making, and independence.

As the epigraph at the beginning of this chapter states, before our tools can shape us, we have to shape them. To do this, we will explore why self-assessment is a natural, human process and how this process connects to equity and growth. To do this, we will explore three paradigm shifts in how we think about assessment and view the role of students and teachers in classrooms. Self-assessment that stands alone, isolated from learning, becomes cumbersome for both teachers and students. Furthermore, self-assessment that occurs after most of the learning decisions have been made does little to nurture growth and authentic decision making. This book is not about helping students evaluate their own work after they have finished. Instead, I present self-assessment as an authentic part of a larger and more complex learning process that holds purpose and meaning for both learners and the educators who serve them.

Three Paradigm Shifts

Effective self-assessment requires a change in who holds agency in the assessment and resulting decision-making processes. While teachers are ultimately responsible for ensuring all students remain hopeful and challenged as they engage in learning goals within classrooms, responsibility for making some of the short-term decisions along the way shifts to students. Furthermore, the assessment processes that drive this decision making happen throughout the learning process instead of at the end. Who students are—their strengths, preferences, and worldviews—is positioned at the center of assessment design and response. Teachers should use assessment to determine exactly where each student is in relation to goals, so students and teachers can co-construct actions and facilitate and support growth. This kind of assessment asks teachers, students, and families to see assessment in three new ways, or paradigm shifts.

1. Assessment as a catalyst for learning
2. Assessment as a collaborative effort
3. Assessment as a state of impermanence

Assessment as a Catalyst for Learning

Effective self-assessment rests on the power of reflection, analysis, and decision making to move learning forward. This kind of assessment requires a shift in how you frame assessment in your schools and classrooms. Instead of assessment holding the sole purpose of labeling and reporting learning after it occurs, assessment becomes a process that invites reflection *while learning is happening* and powers informed decision making about everything from instruction to resources to feedback. In this way, assessment becomes a catalyst for future learning, propelling it forward in intentional and creative ways. This is a paradigm shift.

Self-assessment is only one of several types of formative assessment (assessment that results in action by teachers, students, or both) and, because of the level of responsibility and skill it requires learners to do well, it demands explicit instruction and practice before being implemented within a learning context. As John A. Ross (2006) explains, "There is persuasive evidence, across several grades and subjects, that self-assessment contributes to student learning and that the effects grow larger with direct instruction on self-assessment procedures" (p. 9).

When educators apply this time and effort intentionally, research demonstrates the benefits, even when isolated from other formative assessment strategies. For example, researchers Heidi L. Andrade and Ying Du (2007) surveyed students who engaged in self-assessment strategies and found that students felt more prepared for summative assessment, produced higher-quality work, and had a clearer understanding of what was expected of them as a result. Furthermore, students felt greater motivation and were better at identifying their own strengths and weaknesses within their work.

When students use self-assessment to its maximum benefit, it becomes part of the learning process, moving it forward with each iteration. It doesn't exist outside learning but rather is a process that is difficult to separate from daily decision making, instructional design, and differentiated teaching. It is part of the natural and rich process of learning. In the foreword to *Knowing What Counts: Self-Assessment and Goal Setting*, Andrade (2011) states:

> Blurring the distinction between instruction and assessment through the use of criterion-referenced self-assessment can have powerful effects on learning. The effect can be both short-term, as when self-assessment influences student performance on a particular assignment, as well as long-term, as students become more self-regulated in their learning. (as cited in Gregory et al., 2011, p. 12)

This is the promise of effective self-assessment when it is positioned as a catalysts for learning, and the reason we have to get it right in our classrooms and schools.

Assessment as a Collaborative Effort

Investment can be the result of collaboration or shared decision making. Assessment should reflect students and honor who they are. Decisions, although the result of collaboration, should ultimately relate to and reflect the learners themselves. The following sections explore how collaboration enhances student investment in their own learning, reflects student identities and worldviews, and finally, supports the right amount of challenge to ensure student success and growth.

Collaborative Effort That Enhances Investment

Self-assessment invites students into classroom decision-making processes—to *invest* in their own learning outcomes through collaboration with teachers. Students become partners in learning and instructional design, and classrooms become places of documentation, negotiation, discourse, and problem solving. Most important, classrooms become places of equitable opportunity where student identities (who students are personally, culturally, and socially) and worldviews (understanding of how the world works) are reflected and nurtured. This requires the second paradigm shift—one in which stakeholders view education as a collaborative effort, with all parties making important contributions.

Researcher Tan Ai-Girl (2004) explains, "Teaching engages the teacher's willingness and competence to co-construct spaces of learning to cultivate children's meta-learning skills and competence" (p. 91). This willingness to co-construct, while not always easy, is a necessary precursor to the kind of self-assessment that invites risk taking, supports decision making, and structures safe classroom spaces in which students can experience the consequences of their decisions to revise, relearn, and reimagine different outcomes. These spaces look different from classrooms we may have grown up with, where teachers make all the decisions and students relinquish autonomy in favor of compliance (or not).

A strength of effective self-assessment is that it both causes and reinforces student investment while also supporting a collaborative relationship between teachers and students. Even in those moments when student efforts signal a need for feedback, if that feedback happens in conjunction with self-assessment, students remain in control of decision making.

As explained in *Unlocked: Assessment as the Key to Everyday Creativity in the Classroom* (White, 2019), "Self-assessment is about making decisions and taking action and, without it, the students' efforts and the ensuing results will be less creative and, likely, less satisfactory to the students themselves" (p. 35). It is through the collaboration required during self-assessment that students remain invested in their own learning and make decisions that impact growth and a sense of who they are as learners over time. Assessment expert Tom Schimmer (2014) clarifies the importance of this investment when he explains, "Meaningful ownership isn't just about being responsible for their results. It also involves students becoming meaningful decision makers before and during the learning" (p. 121).

By ensuring students remain in charge of their actions, we are teaching them the true meanings of autonomy, efficacy, and independence. Education consultant Myron Dueck (2014) asserts, "The most important relationship is the one that a student has with him- or herself as a learner" (p. 166). Self-assessment is one of the greatest tools we have at our disposal to help students develop critical relationships with themselves and the world around them.

While self-assessment builds student investment, it also has the potential to build positive relationships between teachers and students. First, almost nothing is more affirming for students than teachers believing their students are capable and competent. When someone believes in us enough to share decisions that ultimately impact us, our relationship with that person is enhanced. It signals an equality and reciprocity that is essential for relationships to flourish. Even when teachers maintain ultimate responsibility for student growth and development, if they communicate the idea that they need partnership in order to experience that success, a different classroom dynamic is established.

As stated earlier, the development of strong self-assessment skills that result in these important outcomes for teachers and learners is not a simple task. Too often, the self-assessment process inadvertently reinforces compliance instead of collaborations—it becomes another handout to complete or another goal to set. This may, in fact, reduce student investment because students perceive actions the educator takes in relation to this kind of self-asscssment as being for the teacher's benefit and not for the learners'.

As assessment experts Cassandra Erkens, Tom Schimmer, and Nicole Dimich (2017) explain:

> Student investment is not about getting students to be compliant; it is about developing students' ability to reflect on their learning in light of a clear learning progression, track their progress, and develop a process for persisting through struggle and growing to achieve more. (p. 113)

Erkens and colleagues (2017) go on to clarify:

> *Student investment* is quite simply the degree to which students invest in their own learning. When people invest in something, they typically devote resources (time, talent, energy, and so on); persist through challenging problems that arise; seek help when needed; and develop confidence in what they are doing, learning, or investing in. (p. 113)

At the center of this commitment to learning lies the student. Students select resources. Students persist through challenges. Students decide when they need help. True investment resides inside an individual, and sustaining this kind of investment yields important outcomes. As researcher and author Carol Ann Tomlinson (2005) explains, "Students' attitudes about learning and about themselves as learners are of great importance in establishing, maintaining, and developing students' commitment to the learning process" (p. 263). True collaboration requires commitment by everyone involved.

A great first step in supporting student investment through self-assessment is to recognize the *qualities* of student investment. In her book *Design in Five: Essential Phases to Create Engaging Assessment Practice*, Nicole Dimich (2015) offers the following list.

When students are invested, they:
- Have language to describe their learning
- Have a clear idea of quality and not-so-quality work
- Take action on descriptive feedback
- Revise their work
- Self-reflect on what the assessment means in terms of their learning
- Set goals based on assessment information
- Make an action plan in partnership with teachers to achieve their goals and improve
- Share their work and plans to improve
- Share their thoughts on what helps them learn and what gets in the way of their learning
- Experience the ways in which the learning is relevant and challenging through assessments, instructional activities, and homework that teachers design (p. 11)

Dimich's list offers a clear path to decisions around self-assessment that support student investment. The important thing to note in this list is that the responsibility for engaging in each item rests with the student. By intentionally teaching students to engage in these actions, we are supporting the development of effective self-assessment skills while nurturing strong assessment relationships and student investment in their own learning. In *Visible Learning for Teachers*, John Hattie (2012) states that these skills in learners make them "assessment capable," and this capability holds critical importance. He describes the necessity and complexity of this work as follows.

> When students invoke learning rather than performance strategies, accept rather than discount feedback, set benchmarks for difficult rather than easy goals, compare their achievement to subject criteria rather than with that of other students, develop high rather than low efficacy to learning, and effect self-regulation and personal control rather than learned helplessness in the academic situation, then they are much more likely to realize achievement gains and invest in learning. These dispositions can be taught; they can be learned. (Hattie, 2012, p. 46)

Collaborative Effort That Reflects Students' Identities and Worldviews

To increase student investment, self-assessment also provides the perfect opportunity to invite collaboration that ensures students are *reflected* in their own learning experiences. This means co-constructing learning environments and contexts that reflect the learners who occupy them—who they are, how they experience the world, what they value, how they live, how they think, and what they wonder. It means that each learner within the classroom holds equal value as a human being, and the strengths of each student are important. Under this collaborative paradigm, students are not marginalized for simply not being the "right" version of a student (for example, extroverted, expressive, quick processor, compliant, quiet). Instead, *all* students emerge as powerful forces in the classroom and important to the collaborative dynamic. This means teachers must intentionally avoid potential biases and be aware of racism, sexism, discrimination, ageism, and any other factor that might contribute to reducing students' abilities to see themselves reflected in their daily learning contexts.

In order to ensure that self-assessment (or any assessment) reflects learners, we must be aware of our own blind spots. Danny Wagner (2017) explains this notion when he describes *cultural humility*: "This is when we recognize that we have biases and limitations to our knowledge regarding another's culture." By acknowledging our own limitations and consequently asking students to share responsibility for goal setting and decision making, we are opening up opportunities for learning experiences to reflect who students are as individuals. Students can select actions during goal setting that reflect their background knowledge, learning preferences, beliefs, and personal strengths. They can seek support from elders, peers, or family members who hold significance for them. They can design learning products or performances that reflect their own interests, values, and ambitions.

When we enter our classrooms with the commitment to reflect learners in our environment, assessment practices, instructional approaches, and learning processes, we can begin to see the critical nature of collaboration through self-assessment. Self-assessment invites teachers to listen while learners share observations, analyses, and goals. This means that conversations will emerge from students in relation to their learning and, in this way, more accurately reflect who they are and what matters to them. This is a powerful shift away from a traditional system that most often reflects the preferences and experiences of the teacher. This student-centered and collaborative approach accepts that educators have as much to learn from their students as their students learn from them.

Collaborative Effort That Supports the Right Amount of Challenge

Last, collaboration through self-assessment invites teachers and students to seek the perfect degree of *challenge* required to maximize rich and meaningful learning. Learners should experience the right balance between confidence and effort and between stretch and support. The OECD (2017) created a handbook that shares seven principles for designing learning environments supporting the well-being of students around the world. The fifth principle captures this need for the right amount of challenge: "The learning environment devises programmes that demand hard work and challenge from all without excessive overload" (p. 25). Together, teachers and students can find this line between healthy challenge and problematic difficulty and between uncovering errors and misconceptions and building successes. Through self-assessment, teachers can develop greater understanding of how to support learners who are struggling and celebrate those who are growing.

The symbiotic relationship between self-assessment and academic growth depends on two things: (1) strength in the complex skill of self-assessment by students and (2) strength in the ways students use self-assessment to grow in content knowledge and skill (articulated by learning goals). Self-assessment, when done well, leads to enhanced learner outcomes and facilitates collaboration and communication between teachers and students to ensure learning experiences are matched to student strengths and needs. Over time, students can become truly metacognitive in the three key ways Dylan Wiliam (2018) describes as "knowing what one knows (*metacognitive knowledge*), what one can do (*metacognitive skills*), and what one knows about one's own cognitive abilities (*metacognitive experience*)" (p. 175). The relationship between these three types of metacognition is the true promise of self-assessment.

Assessment as a State of Impermanence

Any teacher who has spent time with students as they try to learn something new will tell you that it often comes down to mindset—what learners believe about their capacity to learn a new skill or concept. Teachers have witnessed students who dive into a challenge with confidence, not allowing setbacks to prevent them from trying something different, practicing more, or seeking clarification when needed. Teachers have also seen learners quit at the slightest indication of difficulty, throwing their hands up and proclaiming, "I can't!" Both examples show the power of belief in a future state that looks different from the present, indicating whether students think their current state is permanent.

The work of psychologist Carol Dweck has fostered much discourse about how our self-perception impacts our approaches to learning. In the article "What Having a 'Growth Mindset' Actually Means" (Dweck, 2016), she reminds us that a growth mindset (a self-perception that growth or learning is attainable) has to invite mistakes as often as successes: "Organizations that embody a growth mindset encourage appropriate risk-taking, knowing that some risks won't work out." If our assessment systems only emphasize perfection and getting things correct the first time, students will come to believe that their worth lies only in their ability to be right or perfect immediately.

Self-assessment can interrupt this narrative when it occurs early in the learning cycle and invites students to take risks, even when the outcome is uncertain.

Dweck (2016) also speaks openly about the misconception that simply rewarding effort is what growth mindset is all about. She clarifies that developing an optimistic outlook requires learners to reflect on the ways effort may or may not have led to successful goals or desired outcomes. She states, "It's critical to reward not just effort but learning and progress, and to emphasize the processes that yield these things, such as seeking help from others, trying new strategies, and capitalizing on setbacks to move forward effectively." Self-assessment can support students in connecting cause and effect, or effort and growth, while also encouraging a deep dive into the reasons why the growth occurred.

This final paradigm shift requires teachers to allow students to experience the results of both good and not-so-good decisions within the context of an emotionally, socially, and intellectually safe classroom space. It requires a belief that students can make their own decisions and then recover from those decisions when they may not serve their immediate learning needs. Instead of stepping in immediately to "save" or grade students, engage in self-assessment conversations that invite students to interrogate their own actions in relation to goals, and decide whether to continue with the current course of action or switch things up. Moving from a stance of, "You need to . . ." to a position of "Why did you . . . ?" and "How might you . . . ?" can be a paradigm shift in some classrooms.

Ultimately, this stance asks both teachers and students to believe that current assessment evidence is impermanent; that the decisions made today will change the assessment evidence gathered tomorrow. Assessment that supports decision making also supports change and growth. Students can take risks and make mistakes because new decisions emerge from this iterative process. In this way, students can move away from a fixed mindset reinforced through high-stakes assessment toward the notions of curiosity and experimentation. Continuous growth becomes the focus, and self-assessment supports the risk taking required of truly meaningful learning.

This means you have to allow students the opportunity to experience the short-term consequences of their decisions, whether these decisions led them closer to success or further away. Indeed, it is through small failures combined with reflection and change that more meaningful success is ultimately achieved, with greater long-term impact. Researchers Pete Hall and Alisa Simeral (2015) state:

> The most successful individuals today are those who have the ability to reflect—those who are aware of what they know, recognize that what they know is always subject to change, and have the ability to undo and relearn knowledge. Therefore, they are able to revise their belief systems. (p. 47)

Self-assessment is the gateway into this cycle of setting goals, taking action, reflecting on the results of the action, adjusting actions, and setting new goals. This recursive process helps students trust in their own ability to make decisions, decide on approaches, and adjust and recover when it makes sense to do so. Erkens and colleagues (2017) explain the development of this kind of efficacy as follows:

> *Efficacy* requires both belief ("I have the capacity") and action ("I will take risks, even though failure is a possibility"). Efficacy sustains learners as they take risks, make mistakes, modify or adjust their approach or their conceptual understanding, and then attempt another try. (p. 18)

Ultimately, teachers want to support the development of students who will eventually take responsibility for their own growth and learning and who have the resilience to adjust their approaches when needed. You only can accomplish this when you view assessment as the collection of information with regard to learning *in this moment*, and that the evidence will change as students change.

Once you have begun to shift to assessment that acts as a catalyst for learning, that invites a collaborative effort between you and students, and that reflects impermanence or continuous growth, you can begin to take actions to support these paradigms within classrooms and schools. Data notebooks and portfolios are tangible ways to organize and facilitate self-assessment that supports these paradigm shifts. Let's explore these two tools more fully.

The Purpose of Data Notebooks and Portfolios

As explained in the introduction, data notebooks and portfolios are two great ways to collect assessment evidence over time, invite students to analyze this evidence in relation to learning goals, and move toward shared decision making through student goal setting and action planning. However, as great as these tools are for facilitating powerful self-assessment, it is important to also acknowledge that these tools can "go sideways" when they are implemented without careful planning. Erkens (2013) cautions educators in this observation about data notebooks.

> A data notebook is simply a tool and if it is not managed well, it will *not* impact student motivation or achievement in positive ways. There are two important factors educators must consider prior to asking students to create data notebooks: 1) *What promotes growth or change over time?* And, 2) *What are the appropriate ingredients to generate motivation?*

Furthermore, a study conducted by Barbara Meyer and Nancy Latham (2008) finds that despite the overall benefits of portfolios, "the challenges appear to stem from communication about the tool's purpose, use, and capabilities." Clarity about how data notebooks and portfolios can support academic growth while motivating students is essential.

As you explore data notebooks and portfolios, it is important to acknowledge that data and student artifacts (quantitative and qualitative evidence of learning) serve many different purposes in an education setting. Teachers need to collect data and student artifacts for grading and reporting purposes and to inform their instructional decisions, and students need to collect data and learning artifacts to facilitate analysis and goal setting. It is freeing to acknowledge this diversity of purpose and responsibility because it allows teachers to make decisions within their classrooms that serve very specific needs. It also frees teachers from the belief that they need to collect and store all evidence of learning in a gradebook and that this evidence must be used solely for calculating a grade. Data notebooks and portfolios are the students' responsibility (or a shared responsibility in early elementary classrooms), and their data and artifacts of learning should propel self-assessment, metacognition, and goal setting. The notebooks are always available to teachers, but it's students who are best equipped to handle the responsibility for decision making in certain circumstances.

In this way, data notebooks and student portfolios often have overlapping functions and even similar specific attributes. Both involve the collection of artifacts over time that can translate into data (quantitative and qualitative) and reflect the story of learning. Both support students in determining and setting specific learning goals. Both assist learners in retaining and understanding decisions they made while creating specific products and performances, and both can support focused revision and an adjustment of approaches in order to achieve different results. Last, both can promote motivation by making growth tangible and visible to learners.

In essence, data notebooks and portfolios can offer data and learning artifacts that support the following.

- Documentation of strengths, needs, and decisions
- Celebration of growth
- Invitation into analysis
- Prediction of future outcomes and the results of potential decisions
- Inspiration and motivation
- Action for goal setting

The difference between the two tools lies in the focus of the documentation collected over time. Portfolios are often more robust than data notebooks and can contain both quantitative data (in the form of charts, graphs, or tables) and qualitative data (in the form of artifacts of learning, such as assignments, projects, labs, and so on). Data notebooks, on the other hand, tend to focus more specifically on quantative data as the catalyst for reflection, analysis, and goal setting. Neither is better than the other, and which tool you use depends on the intent or purpose.

Because data notebooks and portfolios are intended to be revisited again and again, it is imperative that two things occur. First, it is critical that there is evidence within these tools of students' interaction with and reflection on the contents. Otherwise, these tools will simply become an album of the work as opposed to a catalyst for growth and decision making. Data notebooks and portfolios must be living documents that change over time.

Second, teachers must intentionally monitor whether the notebooks and portfolios support enhanced learner outcomes and whether students experience their engagement in these tools as positive. If students fail to experience growth, as reflected in their data and documentation, they will begin to see the whole exercise as one of compliance and may even feel less optimistic as a result. When students engage with their data notebooks and portfolios, we want them to become familiar with analyzing information that will help them make strong decisions, set relevant goals, and strive for meaning in their daily learning. As Erkens (2013) explains:

> The assessments that are tracked in data notebooks are engaging and meaningful. Literally, the learner can see "worth" in the data he/she is tracking. Most importantly, the culminating data enable the learner to draw healthy and accurate conclusions about his/her own *self*, developing insights into personal strengths and challenges and reflecting on favored content and learning styles. When the learning is provocative, engaging, and self-illuminating, the learner is better able to maintain a commitment to take risks and continue learning.

The same outcomes are important if portfolios are your tool of choice. This book explores various ways to ensure that both data notebooks and portfolios actually enhance students' learning experiences to increase both motivation and depth of skill development and understanding.

Other Self-Assessment Tools

While this book explores self-assessment tools other than data notebooks and portfolios, you can include many of these individual self-assessment tools within data notebooks and portfolios; they do not have to be separate. It really comes down to how you invite students into the self-assessment process, how often students analyze and reflect, and how you decide to collect assessment work and under what conditions.

A data notebook or portfolio has some critical features, as discussed throughout this book, but either can develop in any way that ultimately serves to advance learning, and other self-assessment tools can be part of that process. That being said, there is no requirement that every student has a data notebook or portfolio in every class. In fact, there are times when a simple goal-setting tool is all we need to invite reflection or a simple process for artifact analysis gets the job done. It is for this reason that this book contains discussion questions and examples of simple self-assessment tools that you can add to any learning context.

Regardless of whether self-assessment tools appear in the format of a notebook, a portfolio, or simply attached to a specific product or performance, all tools, when used effectively, serve the following outcomes.

- Foster student interest and investment in the outcome of their own decisions and efforts
- Imply ownership over the outcomes that emerge from educational experiences
- Ask the question, "What next?" and support the relationship between the present and the future
- Nurture diversity and communicate that there is more than one way to approach learning
- Provide the opportunity to clarify what quality learning looks and sounds like and invite learners to linger on proficiency

In the end, all self-assessment tools have to be part of a much broader educational plan. Erkens and colleagues (2019) remind us:

> Tools are only a small part of the overall process teachers must use to develop self-regulated learners in their classrooms. So much depends on the classroom culture, the opportunities to learn from mistakes, and the types of conversations teachers generate about learning as students are immersed in it. (p. 69)

Ultimately, the tool facilitates a learning process, and the process develops the learner. Being clear about how we want equitable learning to look and feel in our classrooms is an important first step.

Where to Start

Sometimes, when exploring a complex process like self-assessment, it is helpful to focus on the very first steps we might take to begin. While the following three steps are not comprehensive, they are a way to begin this process if you are looking for a starting point.

1. Develop personal clarity about how this process serves student learning in the context of your classroom. Be clear about why you are committed to enhancing self-assessment.

2. Begin to craft a plan for how self-assessment might occur during learning, how you might invite students to collect data and artifacts over time, and how you might facilitate moments of reflection. Having clarity about whether you will try a data notebook, a portfolio, or discrete self-assessment tools is a good first step.

3. Begin to imagine how you might include students in the planning and implementation of self-assessment. Without them, self-assessment will fall flat.

QUESTIONS TO GUIDE CONVERSATION AND REFLECTION

On your own or as a part of a collaborative team, consider and discuss the following eight reflective questions.

1. To what degree is self-assessment currently part of my classroom routine? How familiar are my students with this process and how it supports decision making and growth?

2. What form does self-assessment currently take in my classroom? Do students have data notebooks or portfolios? Do they record goals and action plans in an easily accessible place? Does self-assessment primarily occur through conversations?

3. When do students most often get the opportunity to self-assess and make decisions? Do they co-construct daily goals with me? Do they self-assess during the learning process and make decisions while learning? Do they self-assess after a product has been produced or a performance has occurred?
4. What role does self-assessment currently play in lesson and unit planning? Who makes decisions in how classroom experiences will unfold? To what degree does assessment inform decision making?
5. To what degree do students seem invested in their learning? What evidence do I have of their investment? How have I collaborated with students to foster investment?
6. To what degree are students reflected in the learning space? What evidence do I have of this reflection? Would my learners agree with my perception? How might I seek their thoughts and impressions?
7. To what degree is each and every student challenged in my classroom? Is the challenge "just enough" for every learner? Who needs the degree of challenge shifted somewhat, and how do I know? How might I work alongside students to provide the right degree of challenge?
8. To what degree are my learners receiving equitable learning opportunities? How might self-assessment support equity?

CHAPTER 2

Setting Up a Self-Assessment Process and Documenting Learning

There are two fatal errors that keep great projects from coming to life: (1) not finishing (2) not starting.
—*Buddha Gautama*

A first-grade student approaches another student and asks, "Can I have the tablet when you're done? I have a great pattern figured out, and I want to take a picture!" The second student has just used the device to capture a short video clip of her explanation of the pattern she made with natural materials on the sidewalk.

"Yes, I'm almost done," the second student proclaims and then turns to her teacher. "Can I put this in my portfolio?" she asks. "I think this pattern is way better than the one I did yesterday. I want to use this one instead."

"Sure," the teacher agrees. "What makes you think this one is better?"

"I used more materials," the student explains. "This one is more interesting. I explained it in my video." She holds up the tablet.

"When we head back into the classroom, you can upload it to your portfolio," the teacher responds. "Just remember to tag it with the learning goal and the date. Keep yesterday's sample, too. When we reflect tomorrow, you can compare your two samples."

RESPOND TO THE SCENARIO

Answer the following questions using information from the preceding scenario.

- How are students documenting their learning?
- Who is making decisions, and what are those decisions?
- How is the teacher guiding the students?

Imagine you are embarking on an amazing journey. You will travel far, experience challenges, and periodically bask in the glory of hard effort and good results. When engaged in journeys like this, many people document their progress. Whether through photographs, video, or journal entries, you sense that some steps along the way are worthy of capturing somehow—that the struggles and smaller celebrations are as important as the destination. In fact, *through the act of documenting, a profound reflection occurs.* Selecting which photos to take or which words to use to capture complex moments can be as much a part of the journey as the moments themselves.

Hall and Simeral (2015) assert, "We don't learn from experience. We learn from reflecting on that experience" (p. 80). The experiences we have, the documentation of those experiences, and the reflection that occurs as a result are important ways of making sense of our lives. This is exactly why artifacts like data notebooks and portfolios are important—they capture a complex story and invite students to reflect on that story *as it is happening* so the reflection itself impacts the story's outcome. There is a powerful relationship between learning, documentation of learning, goal setting, and self-assessment.

Students' learning stories are personal—they reflect the people experiencing them. When we, as educators, ask students to keep track of their learning in notebooks, portfolios, or computer files, we encourage the creation of artifacts that reflect who students are at moments in time. These artifacts can serve as the foundation of the kind of self-assessment that moves beyond "a thing to do" and into a mechanism that drives rich and complex learning. When we are clear about why we intend to use self-assessment tools, we can begin to plan how to use them in the most powerful ways. Self-assessment is part of a deep learning process that helps individuals explore how their learning occurs over time. When we intentionally plan ways to use it well to nurture learning, we are setting up learners for success. We want data notebooks or portfolios to serve as artifacts of what is most important. Curation of what belongs in data notebooks or portfolios is critical, and teachers and students need to negotiate that curation together.

The setup for using data notebooks and portfolios has to begin by carefully considering student autonomy. It is healthy to co-construct which learning to focus on during documentation and how to collect and organize data. It is important that students and teachers partner in decision making and that the teacher protects the private nature of student progress to ensure emotional safety. (See chapter 6, page 109, for a more detailed discussion on this.)

Data notebooks, portfolios, and self-assessment tools are wrapped up in relationships—between teachers and students and between students and themselves—and these relationships have to be treated with care, from beginning to end. Aspects of data notebooks, portfolios, and other self-assessment tools will remain private for students, while others may become public. Transparency about each is critical in building trust between teachers and learners.

Students need to understand that when assessment *serves* learning (instead of judging it), these data and other forms of documentation occasionally represent less-than-proficient work. In fact, capturing evidence of imperfection is an important part of learning something new. It is through these imperfections that self-assessment can flourish. Students can examine products and performances that are not yet proficient and consider strategies and approaches to get them closer to their goals. This is a shift in the role of assessment and may initially be difficult for students to embrace, especially when they believe that assessment comes at the end of learning and should reflect complete success; anything less than that indicates some kind of failure. It is critical that data notebooks and portfolios contain false starts, searching ideas, and questions. When they don't, they severely limit the potential to develop thinking and generate ideas. Instead, they become transactional, serving only to fill a book and please the teacher. The power of self-assessment is far greater than simply demonstrating compliance and perfection.

In this chapter, you will explore some important considerations for self-assessment, such as providing accessible documentation, offering predictable supports, and establishing a predictable routine. You also will learn practical strategies and tools for setting up the self-assessment process with your students. The chapter ends with clear steps for where to start and questions to guide conversations and reflections with colleagues and students.

Considerations for Self-Assessment

I have started many well-intentioned organizational ideas with students, only to have momentum fizzle weeks after we begin. Binders with color-coded features, journals with daily entries, and mathematics notebooks with consistent reflection have all begun with a strong desire to impact learning. However, like a fitness plan, while having the desire to make a change is an important first step, successful outcomes depend on more than good intentions—there needs to be a structured plan, with check-ins along the way, and daily commitment. Most important, students need relevant purpose and some quick wins to support this purpose, so confidence builds and the effort feels worthwhile. Setting up students for this kind of immediate success with data notebooks, portfolios, and other self-assessment tools begins with preparation.

Data notebooks, portolios, and other formative self-assessment processes depend on features that support predictability and early confidence. Researcher

Dylan Wiliam (2018) asserts that there is much we have yet to learn about formative assessment and how it can impact achievement for students. But he clarifies that we do know some critical things that will "tip the scales in the right direction" (p. 179). Wiliam (2018) reminds us to do the following:

1. Share learning goals with students so they are able to monitor their own progress toward them.

2. Promote the belief that ability is incremental rather than fixed. When students think they can't get smarter, they are likely to devote their energy to avoiding failure.

3. Make it more difficult for students to compare their achievement with others.

4. Provide feedback that contains a recipe for future action rather than a review of past failures (a medical exam rather than a postmortem).

5. Use every opportunity to transfer executive control of the learning from the teacher to the students to support their development as autonomous learners. (p. 180)

To complete these actions successfully, students and teachers need a safe classroom culture, a curated focus, accessible documentation, a strong organizational structure that reflects purpose, predictable supports, and a manageable routine.

Safe Classroom Culture

A safe classroom culture means that students are able to make decisions, set goals, and analyze data without perceived high stakes or public scrutiny. Researchers D. Jean Clandinin and F. Michael Connelly (1995) describe a safe classroom as a place where there is an unspoken understanding that what occurs within the classroom context will be protected between teachers and students. This means that the struggles and celebrations associated with learning are protected from public examination and reporting, unless negotiated by teachers and learners. Therefore, students are free to grow in ways and at times that reflect their own needs. Grading learning prematurely and sharing the resulting scores in a gradebook or on a report card can reduce the culture of safety. When the sole reason for self-assessment is for students to give themselves a grade, the process takes on a different purpose and students may feel more stress as a result.

In addition to a classroom culture of safety, building a shared language with learners about how learning looks and feels is a critical beginning step to engaging in self-assessment and feedback that enhance thinking and ownership. Students need to know that their self-assessment tools will contain learning in progress, and mistakes are opportunities to identify and celebrate because of their potential to stimulate growth. Students have to feel certain that taking risks is important and personal reflection does not come with a penalty. In a classroom culture where risk taking is the norm, both teachers and students have freedom to wonder and try and to succeed and fail. Teachers can model this reality by taking risks themselves—sharing decision making with students, trying new approaches, and then modelling the reflection and adjustments that come afterward.

Students also need to understand the kinds of data and artifacts that will be part of documentation of learning. Knowing whether they will be gathering quantitative data and arranging it into graphs or tables, or whether their documentation will include qualitative representations of learning, is important. Using correct terminology throughout the self-assessment process can be very empowering (for example, teachers of very young children know how powerful new language is and how exciting it is when a learner uses correct terminology).

Table 2.1 (page 22) offers terms and definitions teachers can adopt to accomplish a shared language with students about self-assessment. When and how to introduce these terms will depend on the students' ages and grade levels.

Curated Focus

Having a curated focus means prioritizing skills and knowledge so that by focusing on these priorities (and not on everything), students feel able to achieve success that translates to long-term learning. Data notebooks and portfolios should not reflect everything students learn; they should reflect the *most important* things they learn and the things over which students can exert some decision making. These decisions are best co-constructed by teachers and students.

TABLE 2.1: Building a Shared Language

Term	Definition
Self-assessment	The act of noticing and remembering events, consequences, and actions as related to choices and decisions, and measuring the degree to which the events, consequences, and actions have met a desired result‡
Self-regulation	The act of bringing oneself into a state of order, productivity, or control*
Reflection	Thoughtful consideration of some subject matter, idea, or purpose*
Self-evaluation	To judge one's own actions, products, or performances in relation to specific goals and criteria*
Self-testing	To design specific questions, processes, or tasks that monitor desired progress and then engage in and score the self-designed assessment to ascertain understanding and skill*
Metacognition	Awareness or analysis of one's own learning (skills and knowledge) or thinking processes*
Data	Factual information used as the basis of reasoning, discussion, reflection, or calculation*
Artifact	A tangible representation of skill and understanding; a product, written or representational; any item that reflects learning*
Quantitative	Of, relating to, or involving the measurement of quantity or amount*
Qualitative	Of, relating to, or involving descriptions or judgments of quality*
Documentation	The recording and collecting of documents (artifacts, data, images, written notes) that encourage the development of and reflection about meaningful experiences*
Analysis	A detailed examination of anything complex in order to understand its nature or determine its essential features; a description of relationship between two or more things*
Goal setting	The act of articulating a desired result or outcome in the future†
Action planning	The determining and sequencing of interim actions or strategies that happen in stages in order to address larger goals†

Source: *Adapted from Merriam-Webster, n.d.; †adapted from Cambridge dictionary, n.d.; ‡adapted from White, 2017, p. 112. Visit **go.SolutionTree.com/assessment** for a free reproducible version of this table.

There is room for decisions that reflect individual or group needs as well—perhaps learners collect documentation and data on different priority areas based on co-constructed goals. For example, a teacher might decide that the writing process in English language arts or the problem-solving process in mathematics might reflect important skills that would benefit from continuous documentation, analysis, and goal setting within a data notebook or portfolio. In conversations with students, you might decide to focus on these important goals, with students then making decisions about which aspects of these goals will be personal areas of focus. In English language arts, one group of students might focus on organization for writing, for instance, while another might focus on enhancing language within writing. In mathematics, a group of students may focus on representing their thinking visually, while another group may decide they need to begin by learning to deconstruct complex mathematics problems. In these examples, the teacher decides the broad areas of focus for the portfolio or data notebook, while the students (perhaps in consultation with teachers and after examining their own work samples) decide where they specifically want to begin documentation.

As a result of this decision making, the kinds of documentation students collect may vary for each group. The students who are working on writing organization may document various samples at various stages of development and attach rubrics that describe quality organization. The students focusing on language usage, however, may want to collect quantitative data about the number of adjectives they include in their writing. And students who are working on visual representations of thinking in mathematics may want to focus on documentation that captures their efforts along with descriptive success criteria, while those who are working on deconstructing mathematics problems may decide to collect numerical evidence of the number of times they correctly understood all parts of a complex problem.

These decisions about curation of focus and the kinds of evidence that support this focus can be co-constructed by teachers and students, and even between peers, as they begin to think about what they are going to include in their protfolios or data notebooks. Answering the question, "How will we know when we are getting better?" can be a great catalyst for these important conversations. Following up with, "What documentation should we collect that will allow us to make decisions?" can be a productive second question.

When making curation decisions, it is important to remember that documentation allows students to witness their own and others' learning *in progress*, determine the degree to which they are meeting learning goals, and reflect on and plan for next steps. In other words, documentation is key to successful self-assessment. Establishing documentation parameters means that students collect evidence of problem solving, decision making, and demonstrating learning, so these can be a catalyst to the reflective cycle. Helping students become clear about what will go in their data notebooks or portfolios and how the documentation will support growth is important from the beginning.

Accessible Documentation

In order for data notebooks and portfolios to reach their full potential, it is important that these tools are easily accessible to both teachers and students. The more cumbersome it is to work with the tools, the less often students will want to use them. Many of us can reflect on times we purchased a great tool to use in our gardens or in our homes, only to have it become more trouble than it was worth. The same is true within classrooms. Teachers only have so much time in a day, and working with something that feels difficult or cumbersome is not practical.

Earlier in chapter 1, I explained that you should use data notebooks and porfolios based on practicality and the realities of your specific education context. For example, if computers are not readily available each day or even each week, then digital versions of self-assessment tools may not be the best option. If classroom space is restricted and storage is challenging, then paper versions may need some consideration. If learners are very young, then having them try to navigate three-ring binders may not be the best option. Which versions are most accessible depend on your classroom situation and the ages and skill levels of your students.

Accessibility also refers to how you invite students to document their learning as it is happening. Photography or video capture works well in classrooms in which students have access to and experience with tablets, but if this isn't an option, then documenting learning in this way may not make the most sense. It may be easier to have students draw their ideas or write them in journals instead. If you have students who have visual or auditory impairments, you may need to adapt documentation to reflect these challenges. English learners (ELs) also may need support (for example, vocabulary lists, cloze descriptions) when documenting learning in written, descriptive form. Perhaps for these students, audiocapture or visual representations are more accessible. Every student can engage in documentation, and so you must remove any potential barriers so each student can experience success as independently as possible.

Strong Organizational Structure That Reflects Purpose

Having an organizational structure for data notebooks and portfolios that reflects their purpose means understanding and making decisions about the tools and how students will organize data and reflection. Even the youngest students can engage in collecting, organizing, and developing ownership over their data notebooks or portfolios by personalizing the cover or landing page; building and maintaining a table of contents, glossary, or both; dating and adding titles (or tagging within digital versions) to any data and reflection documents; writing the focus goal clearly on each entry; and selecting the prompts to guide each analysis. Consistency and predictability build confidence and emotional safety (Souers & Hall, 2016; 2019), and so clarifying how each aspect of the notebook or portfolio leads to learning and thinking is critical. How the learning experiences unfold after a self-assessment will, ultimately, determine how well students engage in the process next time. If increased proficiency occurs, they will see a clear connection between formative (self-assessment) and summative processes. Smaller successes over time breed long-term achievement.

Predictable Supports

Student success in creating and sustaining portfolios and data notebooks depends on predictable supports from teachers. In order to offer this support in timely and useful ways, you need to have clarity on the kinds of artifacts and data students will collect and how you will invite learners into analysis and goal setting. It's important to determine whether students should collect and organize quantitative data into charts, tables, or graphs or collect qualitative information through observations, reflections, and anecdotal notes. You also should determine how you can leverage prompts, templates, and other features to support analysis.

For example, the combination of visual representations and written information, or the use of highly-structured prompts and consistent coaching, can enhance the impact of the tools themselves and increase accessibility for ELs and early elementary students (grades K–3). Clarity about the kinds of information to include in notebooks and portfolios, and the kinds of support you offer as these tools are developed over time, can ensure success. By sticking with predictable, simple language, engaging prompts, and clear visual frames, all students can engage in data collection and analysis with greater proficiency and confidence.

Manageable Routine

The Early Childhood Learning and Knowledge Center (n.d.) asserts, "Familiar activities can provide comfort for both adults and children during challenging and uncertain times. Just like adults, children feel more confident and secure when their daily activities are predictable and familiar." In the case of setting up self-assessment processes, having a manageable routine means everyone is clear about when data tracking, documentation, reflection, and goal setting will occur and how often the teacher monitors progress. Students have to tangibly and regularly experience the cycle of documentation and data collection, organization and analysis, reflection and self-assessment, and goal setting and action planning. Self-assessment has to be strongly connected to the learning environment—it has to reflect the kinds of learning students engage in and the processes that yield results. As described in the scenario at the beginning of this chapter, self-assessment is part of the learning journey.

How to Make This Work

When documenting learning and using data notebooks, portfolios, and other self-assessment tools, it's helpful to explore some practical considerations. For example, thinking about how to develop specific self-assessment subskills, make learning visible for students so they can make decisions, and how to create self-assessment tools for students at various grade levels can make self-assessment increasingly successful within the daily business of classroom learning. This section explores the following topics.

- Subskills of self-assessment, which can guide documentation and organization
- Selection of documentation
- Prerequisites for data notebooks and other self-assessment tools
- Setup recommendations for data notebooks and portfolios
- Possible features of early elementary, upper elementary and middle school, and high school data notebooks and portfolios
- Samples and support tools

Subskills of Self-Assessment

I have written at length about the subskills of self-assessment and how helping students develop each skill can contribute to the overall success of complex self-assessment (see White, 2016; 2017; 2019). These subskills (clustered here by relationship within the self-assessment process) are part of effective self-assessment and can, reciprocally, be the reason why some students may find self-assessment challenging in particular contexts. To respond to student needs, you may develop and reinforce each subskill in isolation or in combinations.

- Noticing, remembering, describing
- Relating, comparing, analyzing, connecting
- Predicting, visualizing, imagining
- Empathizing, forgiving
- Decision making, self-regulating
- Organizing, revising, revisiting

For example, you may notice students having trouble identifying strengths within their work, and the reason for this is because they are struggling to forgive themselves for making mistakes. In another case, students may find it difficult to compare aspects of their writing to success criteria because they have trouble noticing attributes within their own essays. Within the context of a data notebook, you may find that students are able to analyze their own data but cannot seem to imagine a different approach that might lead to increased skill or learning. In all these examples, by focusing on the subskills causing difficulty (forgiving, comparing, and imagining), you can enhance each student's ability to make decisions that lead to different outcomes.

Self-assessment tools that lead to rich learning invite students to focus on each subskill, either individually or collectively, through targeted discussions, intentional prompts, and curated processes. Perhaps, before goal setting, we ask learners to share their feelings about not being completely successful in their first attempt at something they are trying to learn. By naming emotions like *disappointment*, *fear*, or *sadness* and acknowledging their existence as part of learning, we can begin to work past challenges.

When developing the subskills of noticing, remembering, and describing, you might ask learners to look at a piece of documentation (writing, for example) and highlight each success criterion as it appears in their work. When students cannot find an example of a particular criterion, they can transfer it to a goal sheet or add it to a list of revisions they need to make. This helps learners develop an increasingly accurate understanding of the quality of their products and performances and where to make improvements.

When students are struggling to imagine different ways of approaching learning (different action steps or strategies), we can offer them a menu from which to choose, or we might engage them in exemplar artifacts and guide them to see new possibilities.

Being aware of the self-assessment subskills allows both teachers and students to make informed decisions as they develop data notebooks, portfolios, and other self-assessment tools, leading to increased skills in self-assessment and academic achievement. When setting up data notebooks or portfolios, it's important to include sections where learners can identify emotional responses to their learning as they occur, make lists of edits and revisions, and document decisions and track the results of those decisions. The subskills also help students curate documentation (artifacts and data) that allow them to:

- Notice, remember, and describe key features of their data, work, thinking, and decision making; these subskills are really important when working with early learners (grades K–3), who are hardwired to think mostly about themselves and their immediate reality
- Relate, compare, analyze, and connect important criteria, actions, and consequences of actions in order to develop a strong understanding between cause and effect
- Predict outcomes of decisions, visualize possible options, and imagine different possibilities
- Empathize with others when they experience successes or challenges and forgive themselves when proficiency does not occur immediately
- Make decisions and self-regulate in order to achieve desired results, both within tasks and across learning experiences
- Organize attempts and data, revisit products and performances, and revise work in order to demonstrate growth

Prompts connected to each cluster of subskills can help students focus on specific aspects of their holistic skill of self-assessment. Figure 2.1 (page 26) offers some sample prompts, which you can use to help students enhance the specific subskills important to overall successful and effective self-assessment. You can use them within a classroom learning context or as artifacts within a data notebook or portfolio.

Documentation precedes analysis, goal setting, and growth. The information in the following sections can help teachers choose the most effective documentation tool for assessment.

Noticing, Remembering, Describing
Prompts include: - Did you notice how your audience responded to your topic? Why? - Did you see other group members stop contributing? Why? - How did you feel when you were able to solve that problem? Why? - What happened last time you tried to work in a group that large? Why? - Did you hear your teacher ask you to listen to instructions?
Relating, Comparing, Analyzing, Connecting
Prompts include: - How do you think those ideas connect? - Which one is more interesting? Why? - Which one feels less enjoyable? Why? - Why might this one _____ when this one _____? - How well does this sample address this criterion? - How might these samples be different? - How might this example help with this one? - How could your strategies this time help you with _____?
Predicting, Visualizing, Imagining
Prompts include: - What do you think might happen next in the story? Why? - Can you imagine a different outcome? - How might you approach this differently? - Where could you add some descriptive language? - Who could offer you some feedback? - Where might you stop to make observations?
Empathizing, Forgiving
Prompts include: - When have you felt this way before? - Why might someone else react in this way? - Who has felt angry when others didn't listen to them? - When might a mistake help us make better decisions later on? - When have you tried something new even when you weren't confident? - How might you forgive yourself when something doesn't turn out how you had hoped it would?
Decision Making, Self-Regulating
Prompts include: - What is your plan to score the next goal? - What could you do to focus when you feel tired? - What makes the most sense right now?

- What decision will you make next? Why?
- If you had fifteen minutes to change this, what might you add?
- Which material will you need?
- What could you do when you feel overwhelmed?

Organizing, Revising, Revisiting

Prompts include:
- How could you organize your timeline?
- Which order seems to support your argument?
- How might you change how you hold your arms?
- When you try again, what will you adjust for better results?
- How much time would you need to make this what you want it to be?
- What might you switch around?
- Who could help you decide which criteria to address?

FIGURE 2.1: Sample prompts for each cluster of self-assessment subskills.

*Visit **go.SolutionTree.com/assessment** for a free reproducible version of this figure.*

Selection of Documentation

Documentation helps students see their current reality and reflect on why that reality exists and whether it makes sense to continue on as is or make some changes. Without documentation, not much else can happen in the way of data notebooks, portfolios, or other kinds of self-assessment. This is why it is so important for students to collect artifacts and data that reflect the most important things. Students interpret what matters in classrooms based on which activities and experiences the teacher prioritizes, and so when setting up self-assessment processes, it is important to give some serious thought to which goals should form the foundation of this work.

Before asking students to collect artifacts and data, think about which learning goals offer the greatest traction for forward momentum across learning experiences. Note that I address goal setting in more detail in chapter 4 (page 71). You might ask yourself:

- Which learning goals are most important for helping learners gain confidence?
- Which goals will serve as the foundation for future learning?
- Which goals are easy to track, based on the learners' developmental readiness?
- Which goals serve learning across content areas and contexts?

These decisions will guide everything else that follows, from the kinds of charts students create to the kinds of goals they set. By centering data notebooks, portfolios, and other self-assessment tools around learning goals (standards, outcomes, competencies, and behaviors), students are able to see their progress over time. This longitudinal picture is important in helping them develop who they are as learners (instead of simply improving specific tasks).

The following are some qualities of documentation that you should consider when setting up data notebooks and other self-assessment tools.

- **Decide which learning goals you will focus on, and then consider the kind of documentation students might collect to track progress on those goals:** For example, if you think the goal of writing strong introductions and conclusions is important, how will you ask students to collect evidence of their growth over time, topic, and purpose? Will students rate themselves using a rubric or teacher-generated assessment? Will they track reader responses to their work? Will they track their use of literary techniques? Will they gather documentation across text types (for example, descriptive writing, narrative writing, and expository writing)? Careful consideration of documentation ensures that it does not always capture the simplest things to track—the simplest things are not always (or often) the most important things. For example, tracking the development of strong introductions and conclusions is best captured through success criteria reflecting quality across text types and purposes as opposed to simply tracking whether an introduction and conclusion are present or absent. Start with the goal and then decide on documentation options.

- **Consider documentation that is developmentally appropriate:** For example, students in grades K–3 may find it easier to document skills that are easy to notice, remember, and track, such as reading fluency data, basic mathematics facts, writing stamina, representing ideas visually, identifying attributes, or brainstorming ideas. Students in fourth grade and beyond will be increasingly ready to document more nuanced skills like playing a game strategically, making inferences, justifying ideas, thinking creatively, and generating solutions to complex problems. Students can document any skill, but not all documentation needs to be quantitative. Having students collect evidence through audio or video files, photographs, anecdotal notes, or some combination of these, can facilitate important analysis as well. Documentation serves as the catalyst for more complex decision making; it is not an end in and of itself.

- **Select documentation that supports evidence-based decision making:** When students reflect on their documentation (data or artifacts), it's vital that they base their inferences about strengths and needs on actual evidence. This is why selecting documentation that forms the basis of data notebooks, portfolios, and other self-assessment tools is so important. It has to offer enough information to students that they can consider the decisions and choices they made and how they might shift those decisions in the future based on evidence.

- **Ensure that the documentation students gather shows evidence of clear and tangible growth:** Students should not examine documentation and be unsure of whether they progressed. This means that numbers should increase, enhanced quality should be visible, and success criteria should be obvious. Any tools, graphs, charts, or descriptors should make the upward trajectory of learning visible.

   That being said, if growth has not occurred, that should be clear to the student as well. If learners are going to make decisions, they need information that tells them what kind of decisions to make. It is for this reason that frequent documentation is important. Interim data, draft work, and images that show learning *as it is happening* will be important in spotting evidence of good or not-so-good decision making.

   Connecting the development of daily learning to larger, long-term learning is vital. Students should understand that the lessons they explore each day connect to something bigger—to richer questions, more complex problems, and authentic and applicable skills. Some of the documentation (data or artifacts) will reflect short-term targets that make up larger goals (standards, outcomes, competencies). Students easily can gather and track this kind of documentation—goals should be immediate, and growth should be rapid. Other documentation will reflect broader, long-terms goals in all their complexity. In this case, the growth is slower and a connection to the smaller targets within the goals is critical.

- **Students should be the primary collectors (or curators) of documentation:** Students have to be in charge of their own self-assessment tools. While teachers certainly guide the process, no one else should be gathering artifacts, recording data, or setting goals for students. A strong reason to include self-assessment in an instructional routine is to build student agency and investment. When we tell students what matters, what they must do, and what it all means, they never have to think for themselves, which fosters an over-dependence on teachers to make all the decisions in the classroom.

- **Documentation should become the catalyst for reflection and action:** Students and teachers will use any documentation collected to reflect on, revise, and plan for future actions and decisions. They should view documentation as evergreen—changing and shifting over time. Evidence of student thinking and decision making should be clear, as students are monitoring results. It is a living artifact filled with the story of learning.

- **Documentation has to be confidential:** Chapter 6 (page 109) explores this topic in greater depth, but it is important that when students collect documentation, they do not suffer shame as a result of what they are collecting. As mentioned at the beginning of this chapter, the importance of a safe classroom culture is paramount. Gathering evidence of success and celebration is easy work, but not all documentation should fall under this category. Students should document and analyze evidence of bad decisions and lack of progress, and this is vulnerable work. Teachers need to reassure students that they will protect their self-assessment tools and share them with others only when it feels safe to do so.

Prerequisites for Setting Up Data Notebooks, Portfolios, and Other Self-Assessment Tools

There are additional considerations before embarking on data notebooks, portfolios, and other self-assessment processes. Clarity and transparency are key. The OECD (2017) handbook referenced earlier clarifies it this way in the sixth learning principle: "The learning environment operates with clarity of expectations and deploys assessment strategies consistent with these expectations; there is strong emphasis on formative feedback to support learning" (p. 25). With this in mind, consider the following prerequisites for planning to use data notebooks or portfolios and other self-assessment tools with clarity and transparency.

- Determine your rationale for asking students to keep a data notebook or portfolio and communicate it to your learners. Consider sharing this information with families as well.

- Determine which templates and processes you will focus on in the beginning and explicitly share them with students. Show examples when appropriate.

- Consider how much freedom and choice students will have in terms of goals and areas of focus, and let students know what to expect and why choice is important.

- Select the way or ways students will collect and store their documentation and reflections. Will they use a notebook or binder, a digital platform or physical folder, or a journal? How to prepare students for self-assessment depends on the form used to organize the documentation. A notebook or binder may need to be divided into sections (according to subject, time period, or stage of self-assessment); a folder might contain subfolders or sections so access to documents is intuitive and easy; and a journal may appear more emergent and organic in form and describe the learning journey as it occurs, much like a story.

- Consider which aspects of the self-assessment process students can personalize and which aspects will be consistent among a cohort of students. Will students choose the organizational structure, or will you, the teacher, prescribe this? Will learners decide which artifacts and data they will collect, or will you decide this? Where do choice and voice reside in this process?

- Estimate how often students will engage in self-assessment (for example, every day, once a week, once a month, at the start of a learning experience, mid-project) and co-construct a schedule or self-assessment map with them. Be sure to share how you've embedded it *within* the learning process (not separate from it), and be careful to avoid presenting it as "a big thing to do."

- Make sure students have a clear understanding of the learning goals (both action-based targets or *I can* statements and success criteria) that serve as the foundation of their documentation, analysis, and goal setting. As mentioned previously, you might direct long-term goals (outcomes, standards, competencies), but you should co-construct short-term weekly or daily areas of focus (short-term goals) with students. Furthermore, you can share or create with students what consistitutes quality products and performances (success criteria) using any number of instructional strategies (for example, sharing exemplars, brainstorming criteria, and sharing non-examples).

It can be helpful to use the phrase, "This means that" to clarify specifically and tangibly what the goals mean in language students understand. For example, for the learning goal, "*I can* make inferences while reading," we might follow with, "*This means that* I can use both my background knowledge and ideas presented in the text to draw my own conclusions about things that are happening but not stated within the text." For students to reflect, they must clearly understand the learning goals.

- Ensure that all instruction and subsequent documentation align with the priority learning goals and are explicitly placed on the documentation (or tagged in digital formats) so students are very clear about the connection between their learning experiences, the artifacts and data collected, or both, and the goals the documentation reflects.

- Depending on how you wish students to display their data, offer instruction and support for creating tables, bar graphs, pie charts, and other ways to organize and display data. If students are recoding raw data, ensure they know how to interpret them.

- Make clear to students that the purpose of self-assessment is to take some kind of action both by continuing what is working well and changing what isn't. It is important that learners know right away that they will be making decisions that affect both their learning experiences (instruction, groupings, practice) and growth. In other words, the assignments and assessments they complete and the documentation they gather offer feedback to teachers and learners.

- Decide how you will seek feedback from students about self-assessment processes. What will indicate success or challenge? How will you gather information about how to shift processes that aren't working and offer more support and guidance when they are required? Is there a critical friend or colleague with whom you might work on developing these processes in your classroom? Sometimes a support person can make reflection far more powerful.

Setup Recommendations

Teachers and students should negotiate together how data notebooks or portfolios look. Some organizational features may be consistent from student to student, and other aspects may be personalized. Setup strongly depends on the purpose of the tool, and so reflecting on why you are engaging in this work with students is important. When it comes to the actual setup, consider the following suggestions.

- Schedule or embed self-assessment into daily lesson plans and longer-term unit plans so students receive regular time and a strong reason to use their data notebooks, portfolios, and other self-assessment tools. Connect the *when* with the *why*. For example, you might choose Monday mornings to establish short-term goals through documentation review and sharing outcomes, standards, or competencies explored. Or perhaps it makes the most sense to take five minutes at the beginning of each class to set goals for the day, with a longer reflection once every two weeks. It depends on what you want to accomplish through self-assessment and the developmental stage of your learners.

- Set a time limit on data-recording and goal-setting sessions so you can move forward with classroom instruction in a timely manner. Build the skills needed to self-assess and set goals so this can happen quickly. Remember, the process takes longer in the beginning and becomes more seamless as students practice self-assessment. Also know that when students are struggling with a learning goal, they need more scaffolding (focus on the subskills of self-assessment as well as content knowledge and performance cues) to guide them in which steps to take and how to get closer to their goals. The further students are from proficiency, the more support they need with self-assessment.

- Label documentation by learning goal or by smaller targets or short-term goals (perhaps with *I can* statements). Have students identify what skill or understanding the data or artifact captures, the specific goal it addresses, and the assessment date for each goal. A single assessment can address multiple targets, goals, or both, but it is best if the assessment itself is organized by target or goal (clearly identified).

- Have students identify whether the documentation represents formative (practice) or summative (for a grade). This could be done through color-coding (for example, formative is shaded blue and summative is shaded yellow) or through symbols (for example, an *F* [formative] or *S* [summative] next to the data point).

- Track work habits and social skills separately from academic data. However, students can track these items if they are priorities.

- Record achievement data by raw score or a clear symbol that represents quality (for example, a rubric level), if possible. This allows students to connect the data directly to their responses and thinking within the documentation.

- Designate a space in the data notebook or portfolio where students can summarize and reflect on any feedback they receive in relation to their documentation (students can make notes directly on the artifact or on a separate template). Feedback is important documentation that can support strong decision making.

- Align self-assessment sessions with current assessments (formative or summative). This ensures instructional momentum.

- Intentionally confer with students individually about their goals. Educational coach Betsy Wierda (2015) states this "should be done within the context of your current instructional frameworks such as guided reading or individual conferencing." This conference can be quick, but making time to check in with each student ensures accountability for both teachers and students. It also allows you to identify and integrate individual strengths and needs into short-term goals.

- Teach students to monitor their own personal goals, if possible, at a designated time during the school day (for example, end-of-day reflection time) or week (Wednesday mornings). This monitoring should include analysis of data or artifacts (strengths and needs), reflection on learning decisions made and their effectiveness in reaching goals, and the decision to continue with a goal or develop a new one.

- Ask students to track data, collect artifacts, or both only when you discuss and connect them to strategies and time for improvement. Remember, action and time are keys to student achievement.

- Avoid praise because "praise can set in motion a student's desire to please teachers as opposed to the desire to please him- or herself" (White, 2019, p. 93). Instead, make affirming statements like, "Tell me more about that," to encourage elaboration and deep thinking while extending interest in student efforts. (For more information on the challenges of praise, see White, 2019, pp. 93–94.)

Features of Data Notebooks and Portfolios That Promote Growth and Learning

Data notebooks and portfolios are about more than just tracking progress—they alter progress to accelerate and enrich it. As a result, any features you include in these tools should facilitate the following five aspects of growth and learning.

1. Setting goals
2. Tracking of indicators
3. Reflecting before and during learning
4. Grounding within clear values and beliefs about learning
5. Connecting to stories and personal meaning

While data notebook and portfolio features are not exclusively for elementary or secondary students (most things can be adapted), there are some ways to adjust the features to suit students' specific developmental needs. As described previously, students in early elementary classrooms (grades K–3) will collect data that is more easily charted and interpreted and focus on goals that are easily tracked, whereas upper elementary, middle school, and high school learners can expand their data and artifact analysis to include more complex skills, resulting in more detailed short- and long-term goals.

Table 2.2 (page 32) offers features you might include in a data notebook for early elementary classrooms, upper elementary and middle school students, and secondary learners.

TABLE 2.2: Features of Early Elementary, Upper Elementary and Middle School, and High School Data Notebooks and Portfolios

	Possible Elementary and Middle School Features		Possible High School Features
Table of contents	This organizational feature can help students find appropriate sections quickly. However, this feature is optional. If tabs or files organize the notebooks, there might not be a need for a table of contents.	**Rationale and table of contents**	In addition to clarifying the notebook organization, the rationale portion can be an opportunity for students to clarify, for themselves, the purpose of the data notebook or portfolio.
All about me	This feature allows students to think about who they are as learners. They can answer questions about themselves and think about their interests and preferences. Early elementary students might represent their ideas visually, adding words as they build confidence and skill with written language. See the "All About Me: Early Elementary" and "All About Me" reproducibles (pages 36 and 37).	**My interests and preferences (Would you rather . . .)**	This feature can invite students to really focus on what works for them in a learning context. It can help them think about making intentional choices when they are offered. See the "What Would You Like to Do?" reproducible (page 38).
My questions	Early elementary students come built to ask questions. Having a designated spot to put questions (or have someone write them for the youngest learners) communicates how important these questions are.	**My dreams and ambitions**	This feature invites students to reflect on their future plans. It allows them to share what matters to them in the long run, an important developmental task for secondary students. See the "My Dreams and Ambitions" reproducible (page 39).
My attendance and work habits	This feature allows students to focus on specific nonacademic areas in which they want to grow. This can include attendance, organization, confidence, teamwork, kindness, and any other habit critical for growth. The selection of these features may be individual (rather than whole class). See chapter 3 (page 45) for examples.	**My attendance and work habits**	This feature allows students to focus on specific nonacademic areas in which they want to grow. This can include attendance, organization, confidence, teamwork, kindness, and any other habit critical for growth. The selection of these features may be individual (rather than whole class). See chapter 3 (page 45) for examples.
My goals	This section is a place where students can store their goal-setting work. They can organize by subject area, by goal, or chronologically. See chapter 4 (page 71) for examples.	**SMART goals and action planning**	This section allows students to store their SMART (specific, measurable, achievable, realistic, and timebound) goals and plan for actions they will take to achieve specific outcomes. This section may contain academic or nonacademic goals. See chapter 4 (page 71) for examples.
My learning story	This feature allows students to document what they are learning and insert artifacts that represent this learning. It can also be a place where learners check off learning goals or targets for a unit of study as they achieve them. See the "My Learning Story Sample: Early Elementary" and "My Learning Story Sample" reproducibles (pages 40 and 41).	**Unit trackers**	This feature can allow students to document things they are learning and insert artifacts that represent this learning. It can also be a place where learners check off the learning goals or targets for a unit of study as they are achieved. See the "Sample Unit Tracker" reproducible (page 42).
My celebrations	This feature allows students to record celebrations and achievements (academic and nonacademic). It is a place for students to acknowledge and document growth. See chapter 5 (page 97) for examples.	**My celebrations**	This feature allows students to record celebrations and achievements (academic and nonacademic). It is a place for students to acknowledge and document growth. See chapter 5 (page 97) for examples.

I used to . . . but now I . . .	This feature invites students to think about decisions they have made and things they used to do and relate them to new understandings and skills. For example, "I used to make my drawings small in my journal, but now I make them bigger and use words, too." See chapters 3 and 4 for examples.	Decisions I've made	This feature invites students to think about decisions they have made and the impact of those decisions on their goals. For example, "I have tried working in a group of more than three people, but I find that working in a group of two or three helps me focus and contribute more." See chapters 3 and 4 for examples.
Feedback for me	This feature gives students a place to collect feedback from the teacher, peers, and other important sources. Students can return to their feedback as often as they want to remind themselves of past efforts. See chapter 4 for examples.	Feedback I've received	This feature gives students a place to collect feedback from the teacher, peers, and other important sources. Students can return to their feedback as often as they want to remind themselves of past efforts. See chapter 4 for examples.
Things I am trying	This section invites students to document processes and strategies they are trying in the classroom and how they feel about these processes and strategies. For example, a student might reflect, "I worked with Emanuel today, and we got more questions done than when I work on my own."	Successful strategies	Students can record strategies they are trying that result in successful outcomes (for example, setting a timer to stay on task).
My data and artifacts	This section is a place for students to track data or collect artifacts over time. The data may take the form of raw scores, graphs, charts, tables, or diagrams. It may be organized by subject area or goal (when goals are cross-curricular). The artifacts may include works in progress and polished versions. See chapter 3 for examples.	My data and artifacts	This section is a place for students to track data or collect artifacts over time. The data may take the form of raw scores, graphs, charts, tables, or diagrams. It may be organized by subject area or goal (when goals are cross-curricular). The artifacts may include works in progress and polished versions. See chapter 3 for examples.
My self-assessments	This feature is based on specific tasks, experiences, or performances and invites students to reflect on success criteria and articulate strengths and needs. Students may also have a place to explain their self-assessment and back it up with evidence. See chapters 3 and 4 for examples. In the early years, as students are developing the complex skill of self-assessment, they may focus on one or more of the subskills (see chapter 1, page 9) to practice and reinforce these important skills as part of becoming a proficient self-assessor. For example, students may reflect on their efforts in noticing and describing events as they occur or showing empathy to others. As students get older, these subskills will combine into more complex self-assessment in relation to long-term learning goals (outcomes, standards, or competencies).	My self-assessments	This feature is based on specific tasks, experiences, or performances and invites students to reflect on success criteria and articulate strengths and needs. Students may also have a place to explain their self-assessment and back it up with evidence. It is a place to acknowledge emotional responses to assessments as well as begin to make tangible decisions for the future. See chapters 3 and 4 for examples.

*Visit **go.SolutionTree.com/assessment** for a free reproducible version of this table.*

Where to Start

Sometimes when exploring a complex process like documentation and setup, it is helpful to focus on the very first steps we should take to begin. While the following five steps are not comprehensive, they are a way to begin this process if you are looking for a starting point.

1. Openly discuss the role of self-assessment and goal setting in learning. Draw parallels to self-assessment that happens outside school (for example, while playing sports, playing video or other types of games, cooking or baking, planning a visit with friends or family, or organizing a vacation).

2. Explicitly invite students to attach learning goals to artifacts and data. Make the learning goal and success criteria visible on every artifact. Work toward evidence of learning as opposed to work to be completed (two different paradigms). Select a few priority goals to focus on in the beginning. For example, students might include a couple of science lab reflections in their portfolios. The goals of representing data and drawing conclusions may be attached to both samples as areas of focus. Subsequent analysis and goal setting would also focus on these two priority goals. Other skills would be applied within these reflections, of course, but these two goals are the ones that receive time and attention because they are broadly transeferreble across science topics.

3. Invite students to document their learning as it happens. Experiment with video, audio, and photographic documentation. Depending on your school's policies, learners might have their own devices on which to capture their efforts, or you may have one available for educational purposes. This can invite conversations about appropriate ways to share information, access copyright laws, and capture thinking. Also, encourage students to keep drafts, thinking pages, outlines, and so on. Describe the importance of these kinds of documents in learning to build assessment skills.

4. Begin by asking students to reflect in a designated spot (for example, notebook, digital file, or journal). Get them used to thinking about their decision making and making the time and space for it in their daily learning.

5. Work on developing the self-assessment subskills. Name them, use them in lessons, and encourage students to see how they might be using these subskills and why.

TOOLS TO SUPPORT SELF-ASSESSMENT

The following templates and tools can provide a framework for setting up your self-assessment process and beginning documentation. As indicated, some templates and tools are more appropriate for early elementary classrooms and some are better for upper elementary and middle school or high school.

> **"All About Me: Early Elementary" reproducible (page 36):** This tools invites students in grades K–3 to reflect on their strengths and preferences.

> **"All About Me" reproducible (page 37):** This tool invites upper elementary and middle school students to reflect on their interests and preferences.

> **"What Would You Like to Do?" reproducible (page 38):** Use this tool with high school students as a way to clarify preferences and strengths.

> **"My Dreams and Ambitions" reproducible (page 39):** This tool invites high school students to reflect on their future.

> **"My Learning Story Sample: Early Elementary" reproducible (page 40):** This tool offers an example of a way for grades K–3 students (with help from an adult, if needed) to monitor and celebrate short-term skill development.

- ➢ **"My Learning Story Sample" reproducible (page 41):** This tool offers an example of how upper elementary and middle school students might monitor and celebrate short-term skill development in relation to longer-term goals.

- ➢ **"Sample Unit Tracker" reproducible (page 42):** This tool offers a process by which teachers and students can work together to clarify the goals for a unit and also specify what each goal looks and sounds like. Students can then monitor and celebrate attaining these goals as the unit progresses.

- ➢ **"Monitoring My Learning" reproducible (page 43):** This tool, appropriate for any grade level, invites students to reflect frequently and document any learning they feel has taken place. It reminds students that learning represents new skills or understanding and not things they can already do. This tool can serve as a catalyst for decision making or celebration.

- ➢ **"Documenting and Reflecting on My Learning" reproduble (page 44):** You can use this tool with students in grades 4–12 to curate samples of learning (products and performances) that represent specific strengths and needs to include in a data notebook or portfolio. These samples can help learners set goals for the next unit. After choosing samples, students can respond to specific reflection questions.

QUESTIONS TO GUIDE CONVERSATION AND REFLECTION

On your own or as a part of a collaborative team, consider and discuss the following eight reflective questions.

1. How often are students collecting documentation of their learning at various stages and using it as a catalyst for conversations about decision making?

2. How could I expand the kinds of documentation students collect?

3. How does it make sense, in my classroom, to organize the data and artifacts students create so they can revisit them as part of advancing learning?

4. How might I explain data notebooks and self-assessment to students? How could I frame this conversation?

5. What changes might I need to make in my instructional routine to create space and time for self-assessment?

6. Which aspects of self-assessment are most important in my classroom? What do I want to include? What is less important to me and my students right now?

7. To what degree are my learners comfortable with each of the subskills of self-assessment? Are some subskills a strength for my students? Are there some in which students clearly need additional practice and support?

8. How comfortable are my students with taking risks, making mistakes, and turning initial failure into productive learning? To what degree do I have a classroom culture that supports authentic self-assessment, decision making, and goal setting?

All About Me: Early Elementary

Name: _____ Date: _____

Write or draw your ideas about yourself as a learner in the spaces below. Work with a partner if you like.

This is me	These are things I like at school	These are people who can help me learn	These are some questions I have

These are things I like to learn about	These are ways I like to learn	These are places I like to learn	This is what I am good at already

Student Self-Assessment © 2022 Solution Tree Press • SolutionTree.com
Visit **go.SolutionTree.com/assessment** to download this page.

All About Me

Name: _____ Date: _____

Complete the prompts in each column to describe yourself.

All About:				
Words that describe me	**My favorite books or stories**	**Things I like to do with my friends**	**My favorite activities when I'm alone**	**My favorite activities when I'm with my family**
			Very favorite activities: Other activities:	
I'm very interested in or good at . . .	**Things I'd like you (or need you) to know about me**	**My hopes and dreams for myself**	**The easiest ways for me to show what I know**	**One thing I would like to do better**

Shhhhh! My greatest fears are:

What Would You Like to Do?

Name: _____ Date: _____

Check the box next to the activities you participate in to demonstrate your interests and learning preferences.

☐	Read an informational text	☐	Examine an infographic or a chart
☐	Work in a group	☐	Work on my own
☐	Talk through an idea	☐	Create a concept web or map
☐	Present information to the class	☐	Share information using tech
☐	Receive data to help me track my growth	☐	Hear a story
☐	Give others feedback	☐	Receive feedback
☐	Create a list	☐	Draw a picture
☐	Work at a table	☐	Work on the whiteboard
☐	Be assigned a topic	☐	Be invited to choose a topic
☐	Work with overhead lights on	☐	Work by a window
☐	Make a video	☐	Collect and organize images
☐	Read informational texts	☐	Read fiction
☐	Complete homework at school	☐	Complete homework at home
☐	Lead a group	☐	Be led within a group
☐	Share ideas by talking	☐	Share ideas through writing
☐	Write a research paper	☐	Create a poster
☐	Work in a silent room	☐	Work amid activity
☐	Use my imagination	☐	Change something that exists
☐	Ask questions	☐	Provide answers
☐	Learn step by step	☐	Start with the big idea
☐	Work with short deadlines	☐	Plan to manage my own time
☐	Work with a friend	☐	Work with someone new
☐	Reflect on my own	☐	Reflect with a partner

Student Self-Assessment © 2022 Solution Tree Press • SolutionTree.com
Visit **go.SolutionTree.com/assessment** to download this page.

My Dreams and Ambitions

Name: _____ Date: _____

List your dreams and ambitions and some of the things you need to do to make these dreams a reality.

My dreams and ambitions for the next year include:

Things I need to do to make these dreams a reality:

My dreams and ambitions in the next five years include:

Things I need to do to make these dreams a reality:

My dreams and ambitions in the next ten years include:

Things I need to do to make these dreams a reality:

Student Self-Assessment © 2022 Solution Tree Press • SolutionTree.com
Visit **go.SolutionTree.com/assessment** to download this page.

My Learning Story Sample: Early Elementary

Teachers and students work together to monitor and check off learning students have accomplished.

- ☐ I can count forward to ten.
- ☐ I can count to ten forward and backward.
- ☐ I can say a number and then say the numbers that come before and after that number.
- ☐ I can write the numerals 1 to 10.
- ☐ I can use materials to show the value of numbers one to ten.
- ☐ I can draw an example of what each number represents.

Which of these skills was easy to learn?

Which of these skills was hardest to learn?

What helped me learn?

Who helped me learn?

My Learning Story Sample

As you progress through this unit of study, use reflection time to keep track of the skills and knowledge you are developing. Identify evidence in your data notebook or portfolio to support your claims.

	I can apply defensive skills when playing a game or sport.
Enriched Understanding	I can: ☐ Apply defensive skills across multiple games ☐ Relate the defensive skills of one game to another ☐ Create a defensive skill plan to share with others ☐ Be flexible when applying defensive skills (and adjust as needed)
Proficient	☐ I can apply defensive skills. This means: • Thinking ahead and predicting outcomes • Considering my position in relation to others and moving when needed • Being clear about the goal of the game or sport and actively working toward that goal • Putting the needs of my team ahead of my own desire to score, shoot, and so on
Exploring	I can: ☐ Learn the rules of the game and be clear about the end goal ☐ Imagine a variety of outcomes in a given situation ☐ Practice moving into various defensive positions in a timely fashion ☐ Play as part of a team rather than as an individual—relate my actions to those of others ☐ Practice the game-specific defensive skills (sending and receiving, positioning, skillfully moving) ☐ Learn from my mistakes ☐ Take risks
Building Readiness	I can: ☐ Describe the difference between defensive and offensive play and why both are necessary ☐ Explain the roles of each position in a game ☐ Know how to play the chosen game (rules, equipment) ☐ Move skillfully and quickly ☐ Be patient ☐ Notice what others are doing ☐ Be part of a team (kindness, forgiveness, encouragement, common goal)

Student Self-Assessment © 2022 Solution Tree Press • SolutionTree.com
Visit **go.SolutionTree.com/assessment** to download this page.

Sample Unit Tracker

Name: _____ Date: _____

Complete this chart together with your teacher while examining evidence in your data notebook or portfolio.

Unit Learning Goals and Targets	"This Means That" Statement (Student-Accessible Description of the Goal)	Met	Not Yet Met

Student Self-Assessment © 2022 Solution Tree Press • SolutionTree.com
Visit **go.SolutionTree.com/assessment** to download this page.

Monitoring My Learning

Name: _____ Date: _____

At the end of each day, reflect on what you learned. Record only those things that are new learning (not the things you can already do). Use this chart to describe what you have learned.

Date	What I Learned Today

Student Self-Assessment © 2022 Solution Tree Press • SolutionTree.com
Visit **go.SolutionTree.com/assessment** to download this page.

Documenting and Reflecting on My Learning

Name: _____ Date: _____

Select samples from this unit to include in your data notebook or portfolio. These samples will help you set goals for the next unit. Look through your artifacts, products, and performances from this unit, and choose the following samples for your notebook or portfolio. Using a sticky note or tag, answer the prompts for each sample you choose.

- A work that you would like to do over again
  How would you change it if you could? Which skills should you apply?

- A work that shows growth in one or more skill
  How can you give evidence of this growth?

- A work that had some hard parts and some easy parts
  Which parts were which? How did you deal with the hard parts?

- A work that has some potential but needs a little more attention
  Where do you need to focus some time and why? Which skills do you need to apply?

- A work that you stuck with even though you didn't want to keep working on it
  Why was this work so tough? How did you keep working on it, even when it was hard to do so?

- A sample that you are really proud of
  What do you want people to notice about this sample? Which goal or goals does it reflect?

- A sample that shows you took a creative risk
  What did you try, even though you weren't sure how it would turn out?

- A sample that shows critical thinking
  How did your thinking change as you worked through the chosen sample?

- A sample you created as a result of collaboration with others
  How did other people contribute to this work?
  How did working together make this work better? What was hard about working together?

- A sample that you enjoyed doing
  Why was this sample so enjoyable? What parts did you like the best?

Student Self-Assessment © 2022 Solution Tree Press • SolutionTree.com
Visit **go.SolutionTree.com/assessment** to download this page.

CHAPTER 3

Engaging in Analysis and Reflection

Learning can link the rare moments of sudden understanding with gradual change through practice, the longitudinal epiphanies.
—Mary Catherine Bateson

"For today's reflection and intention setting, we are going to focus on the data and artifacts you have collected over the last two weeks. I am inviting you to take a broader look at your learning decisions in this mini-unit. I would like you to think about how you approached your learning as we explored poetry. How did you feel coming into this unit? Were you excited about poetry or were you anxious?"

The teacher pauses and lets students process those two questions. He then continues, "Please turn to an elbow partner and describe how you felt about this unit before we began and how your feelings might have changed as we explored different kinds of poetry. Describe your learning story to your partner."

The teacher wants students to think aloud before they begin their more formal written analysis. For some students, he knows that talking is a way to process ideas and prepare to write. For others, listening is a powerful learning catalyst.

The students turn to their partners and establish who will go first. They seem excited to share their feelings. The teacher watches the learners carefully for signs of hesitation within pairings. He doesn't want to step in if they are able to engage in the task, but every now and then he has to join a pair and help the partners establish a collaborative relationship. They are well into the semester, and the teacher doesn't see evidence of hesitation today; students are increasingly comfortable with these kinds of conversations.

Once students have had the opportunity to share their stories, the teacher calls them back to focus on the next instructions. "In this mini-unit, you documented more than one thing." He gestures to a list he wrote on the board. "You created a bar graph to collect data on the volume of figures of speech you applied within your own poems for each type of poetry we studied. You also collected your brainstorming sheets and draft versions of your poetry. I then asked you to select two poems that you felt demonstrated the greatest improvement from your first brainstorm to your final version. You should have a record of your daily writing goals in your data notebook. Please take a moment and locate each of those artifacts and data in your notebook. Also, find the list of success criteria I handed out at the beginning of this unit."

The teacher pauses and waits for students to find the artifacts, data, and success criteria. When they are ready, he continues, "Today, I would like you to use all the documentation from this unit to reflect on your growth and learning over the past two weeks. Consider where you began and where you ended up in your own confidence and skill in writing poetry. I am going to hand out a template with four prompts on it. Please take some time to consider the questions carefully and offer your thoughts. I am asking you to identify your strengths and areas in which you would like to continue to focus and improve. I also am asking you to reflect on the goals you had throughout this unit and the decisions you made that got you closer to your goals as well as those that took you further from your goals. As always, this reflection should include both writing decisions and decisions around managing your time and workload. Please remember that for each of your responses, you will need to support your ideas with evidence, either from your data or your artifacts."

RESPOND TO THE SCENARIO

Answer the following questions using information from the preceding scenario.
- What role does documentation play in this scenario? In what ways do artifacts and data lead to analysis and reflection?
- What decisions are students making, and how do teachers have them reflect on those decisions?
- What is the role of the teacher in this scenario? What is the role of the students?

This chapter explores the skills of *analysis*, a "detailed examination of anything complex in order to understand its nature or determine its essential features" (Merriam-Webster, n.d.) and *reflection*, the thoughtful "consideration of some subject matter, idea, or purpose" (Merriam-Webster, n.d.), including causes and consequences of actions and decisions. Students might apply these skills examining individual assignments or learning experiences and thinking about strengths, needs, and plans for their next iteration of learning. They may also apply these skills to a collection of artifacts or data sets that represent learning over a longer period of time (perhaps located in data notebooks or portfolios), with goals emerging from this process feeding the end of a unit or the next unit of study. Learning to analyze what these samples are showing about progress in relation to both short- and long-term goals is an important part of self-assessment and overall growth. For example, after a mini-unit on physical reactions, students may analyze and reflect on artifacts or data that indicate their skills of hypothesizing and drawing conclusions. Learners may decide whether there is evidence that these skills are proficient or whether they need to enhance these skills in their next mini-unit on chemical reactions.

Artifact and data analysis of samples that do not belong to you can be a highly objective process, but when it's connected to self-assessment and goal setting (and your own samples), it can get a little more personal. This personal element requires finesse when teaching students to analyze their own documentation. Allowing time to process emotional responses before moving into goal setting is important. Clear protocols can help students manage complex information and feelings and connect cause and effect more readily.

Furthermore, when you invite students to analyze their own data or artifacts, you are asking them to connect what they feel about their efforts (both their emotional responses and perceptions) with what the evidence is showing in their artifacts, products, or performances. Research shows the possible cognitive bias associated with the ability of a person (students included) to accurately assess their own strengths and deficits (see Jonathan Jarry's 2020 article, in which Jarry offers a critical response to the original Dunning-Kruger effect research, which maintains that people often greatly overestimate their own knowledge or competence in certain areas or domains). Jarry explores the possible ways interpretations of the Dunning-Kruger effect have been oversimplified and misconstrued by the popular media. Whichever way you land on this issue, this is a great moment to distinguish between self-assessment and self-evaluation.

Note that the intention of this book is not to have students grade themselves (self-evaluation). This is the professional responsibility of the teacher. Rather, when students analyze and reflect on their efforts in relation to specific goals and success criteria, they are doing so as a way to offer insight about the next instructional steps. In fact, the purpose of analysis and reflection within self-assessment is to bring students closer to an accurate understanding of their current levels of proficiency and more closely align their perceptions with reality.

Analyzing documentation, whether quantitative or qualitative data or artifacts, requires students to possess three complex skills.

1. Students must be observers—they must notice all the information needed for analysis and not simply focus on a single photograph, number, or object.

2. Students need to relate one thing to another, describing similarities, differences, and cause-and-effect relationships.

3. Students must remember and then connect the documentation they are analyzing to decisions they might have made that led to the results they observe.

Explicity teach these three skills through modeling, practicing, and correcting, when necessary. In fact, making time to formatively assess students' ability to analyze data is part of establishing a strong self-assessment process. Dimich (2015) articulates the value of this level of student engagement in data and artifact analysis when she explains:

> The key to tracking is to target a standard or skill that occurs over time. As students engage in assessments and practice that targeted skill, such as data analysis, it becomes a visual representation students can use to reflect on how they are progressing. Students often find the visual an effective way to begin to make connections to their work and their learning. This tracking provides information for setting goals and making plans to improve between assessments. (p. 99)

When students are able to connect the decisions they make and actions they take while learning to tangible data, artifacts (assessment of products or performances), or both, they can be part of the instructional process often reserved for teachers. This kind of formative assessment invites a co-construction of choices and approaches that support learning and the overall educational experiences of both teachers and students.

There are a number of steps students must take to progress from documentation through analysis to goal setting and action planning. Chapter 2 (page 19) explored documentation, and this chapter focuses on the skill of analyzing data and artifacts of learning to identify strengths and needs based on explicit success criteria. Once this analysis occurs, imagining different decisions and outcomes follows.

During data and artifact analysis, students should get the opportunity to engage in some or all of the following activities.

- Collect information (data and artifacts) and include early drafts, brainstorming, and other evidence of learning as it develops, when possible. Relating this early evidence to later data, products, or performances will help students see their growth in a tangible way.
- Organize data and artifacts in a way that makes patterns and relationships clear. Practice writing, drawing, making tables, diagrams, and graphs.
- Practice data description and interpretation, using appropriate and accurate language (provide support as needed, perhaps for early elementary learners and ELs).
- Record questions students may have about what they are noticing in their data and artifacts. For example, a student might notice that the accuracy of their solutions to mathematics problems is not increasing, and ask, "How can I get more correct answers?" or "Why did I start my solutions well but still end up with the wrong answer?"
- Record ideas and evidence related to relationships they are considering, connections they are making, and decisions they are contemplating.
- Identify strengths in their documentation and reflect on the reasons for these strengths.
- Identify areas needing improvement to advance their learning; reflect on the reasons for the challenges they are seeing. Celebrate their mistakes as opportunities to grow and make different decisions.
- Begin to note possible actions they may take (to be formalized later).
- Reflect on the effectiveness of past actions, based on longitudinal data and comparing older artifacts with newer ones.
- Connect past goals to current documentation.

If teachers opt to use data notebooks, portfolios, or some other method of gathering and analyzing documentation over time, it is important that students collect work and data that reflect various stages of proficiency. By doing this, students come to understand that the purpose of self-assessment is to empower learning and not simply to document it once a learning experience has ended.

Beth Leffler and Brenda Crauder (2011) capture this characteristic within data notebooks when they write, "Mistakes are welcome opportunities to learn and grow. Students are encouraged to continually build upon items in the notebook, not erase or tear them out" (p. 59). In this way, the notebooks and other self-assessment tools become representations of a learning journey and not just a photograph of the final destination.

It is possible that students who are engaging in analysis and reflection of early learning samples, or who are at the beginning stages of developing specific skills and understanding, might find it more challenging to reach an accurate analysis without instruction, support, and mentoring. This is simply a case of "not knowing what they don't know," and is common when students are learning complex skills and building deep understanding. This is why the role of the teacher is so critical during self-assessment. Teachers are often masters of content and skill, and they are the best people to guide students in learning how to analyze their documentation.

In this chapter, you will explore several considerations for self-assessment as related to analysis and reflection, including how to engage students in effective and meaningful feedback. You also will learn strategies for how to make analysis and reflection work for your students, such as ways to analyze a single artifact or compare multiple artifacts or data sets. At the end of the chapter, you will find practical templates and tools to help you and your students engage in analysis and reflection, along with steps for where to start and questions for conversation and reflection with colleagues and students.

Considerations for Self-Assessment

Teachers engage in artifact and data analysis regularly to make instructional decisions, group students by learning need, clarify interventional supports, and adjust unit pacing, as required. Formative assessment information, in particular, invites regular analysis by educators in service of the construction of effective learning experiences. However, there are times when it is prudent for teachers to increase transparency and build shared ownership for some of these decisions with learners. Marnie Thompson and Dylan Wiliam (2007) share the importance of this co-construction when they write:

> Teachers cannot create learning—only learners can do that. What teachers can do is create the situations in which students learn. The teacher's task, therefore, moves away from "delivering" learning to the student and towards the creation of situations in which students learn. (pp. 5–6)

When teachers and students share learning decisions, they increase their chances of creating effective learning contexts. By the time we send students out into the world, we hope they develop not only the knowledge and skills various academic learning goals require but also the ability to make learning decisions that serve them for the rest of their lives.

In their article "The Power of Feedback," John Hattie and Helen Timperley (2007) offer clarifying information that can have an impact on how we might approach data notebooks and other self-assessment tools. If we reframe self-assessment as a process whereby students give themselves feedback through the analysis of assessment information (gathered through artifacts and data), we can consider how Hattie and Timperley categorize feedback. They propose that there are four kinds of feedback, with varying effects on learning.

1. **Personal-level feedback:** This kind of feedback focuses on the students themselves. For example, in a self-assessment context, this might sound like, "This grade proves that I am smart," or "This test shows that I can't do mathematics." This kind of feedback is counterproductive and implies fixed ability. It also indicates that students are connecting their value to their scores or results.

2. **Task-level feedback:** This kind of feedback focuses on a specific task with the intent of improving the product or performance. In a self-assessment context, this might sound like, "To fix my solution to this problem, I need to correct this part of my calculation," or "My conclusion for this essay needs a clearer resolution to this key question." This feedback is helpful in improving the quality of a specific task, but it has limited long-term impact on learning from one task to the next. When students are at the beginning stages of learning a new skill, this feedback is a great place to start, but it is important to begin to transition into the next kind of feedback.

3. **Process-level feedback:** This kind of feedback focuses on the processes applied during a particular learning context. For example, when students are self-assessing, reflecting, and goal setting, this might sound like, "When I was brainstorming ideas for my science project, I

needed to remember to include all categories of mammals. I will want to have those categories handy when generating ideas," or "I liked drawing my thinking before writing words because then I remembered what I wanted to say better." This kind of feedback has a high level of impact because it narrows the learner's focus to why their work may have fallen short by inviting students to consider decisions they have made in approaches to learning and the degree to which those decisions had a positive impact on the final outcome.

4. **Self-regulation feedback:** This kind of feedback requires students to monitor and respond to their own learning, considering how they might apply current skills and strategies to long-term efforts. Self-regulation feedback addresses students' understanding of themselves as learners, and not just the current task. This might sound like, "When I am writing, I find I can produce more when I take short body breaks every forty minutes. It seems to allow my brain time to reset so I can do a better job of making my ideas clear," or "It helps me to have mathematics materials handy when I am working through fractions problems because then I can grab things and manipulate them when I need to see a problem more clearly." This kind of feedback has a strong connection to optimal learning in both the short and long term.

When it comes to analysis, this research helps ensure that when we are teaching students to engage in analyzing their own data and artifacts, we move beyond simply focusing on the current assessment or task toward building an understanding of effective processes and self-regulation strategies that serve learners over time and across learning experiences. By connecting analysis to goal setting, students can see the impact of their decisions on both the tasks they are focusing on in the present moment as well as future learning. This helps students move beyond collecting and graphing data as a task and toward reflecting on how these data or artifacts came to be and their relationship to the goals they're exploring.

When students take an active role in analyzing documentation, they are engaging in the same processes as teachers when developing feedback. When students receive feedback from teachers in combination with feedback generated from their analysis, they have the opportunity to be deeply involved in decision making. This is why the timing of the analysis is so critical. This process needs to happen *during* learning so there is ample time to respond to what these data indicate as a need.

As you develop the skill of analysis with students, it is helpful to be clear about what strong analysis looks and sounds like. If analysis is successful, students should be able to:

- Identify their strengths both within a task, in terms of decision making and strategies, and from task to task, as strong learners

- Identify their needs by goal, by target, by criteria, and by resources (time, supports, tools)

- Reflect within their data notebooks or portfolios in relation to assessment information, including analyzing relationships, identifying anomalies, and designing responses

- Identify work samples that address specific targets and quality criteria; link evidence to goals

- Offer feedback to others based on the available samples and criteria but also based on their own experiences as learners

- Apply feedback from others; make decisions that connect to goals, evidence, and experience; apply intention to action

Some students may struggle with aspects of analysis. For some, the skills of noticing, comparing, and relating will be difficult. For others, the emotional aspect of analysis will be the greater challenge. For example, this process may cause some students to feel overwhelmed or confused about their lack of proficiency, while others may rely on their data to affirm their personal value. There may even be learners for whom cultural customs challenge their willingness or ability to engage in aspects of analysis. Students may be uncomfortable reflecting on their strengths, for example, because they perceive it as bragging. For this reason, we have to attend to the whole student in the analysis process, being open with learners about what we are hoping to achieve and why. We may need to negotiate how analysis might happen, so students feel supported and reflected in the process.

How to Make This Work

There are many ways for students to engage in analysis. Sometimes you may want students to analyze a single artifact (test, essay, video, photograph, solution, response) and consider what it tells them about success in relation to criteria. Other times, you may want students to think about decisions they made and strategies or processes they used to arrive at the work under consideration. As students progress in their learning, you may ask them to compare two or more artifacts or look at data in relation to more than one attempt at a skill for patterns and anomalies. At the same time, you may invite them to track their progress on targets within complex learning goals in a unit of study. All these forms of analysis focus on relating the current state to future goals and making decisions about next steps.

As stated earlier, it is critical to prioritize where students should spend time on analysis. This process takes time and requires a commitment to revision and reflection. It would be impossible to engage in this level of analysis for every learning experience that occurs in the classroom. Only the most important goals should form the basis of formal analysis.

Also keep in mind that analysis of artifacts or data can feel challenging when the process is new, so modeling analysis as a class is helpful. Furthermore, ensuring student responses will be offered in an emotionally safe way is critical. It would not be appropriate to have students share their analyses with others, for example, unless teachers and students first establish a supportive classroom climate. In this safe classroom space, students understand that artifacts and data that reflect low proficiency are not only possible but required, and they should withhold judgments about their peers' abilities and efforts.

The following are the various kinds of analyses possible within data notebooks and other self-assessment processes. Underneath each type are prompts to guide students through analysis. It is important to offer only a few prompts to students. Otherwise, the analysis can easily become time consuming and overwhelming. It is helpful to begin any analysis session with these questions: "What learning goal (or goals) are we focusing on today?" and "What are we trying to learn from our analysis today?" These questions ensure students' focus is very specific during self-assessment and goal setting.

Analyzing a Single Artifact

For this option, students should have the artifact in front of them, as well as prompts and success criteria. Students can record their analysis in their data notebooks or portfolios. They can also complete this process verbally, or record and transcribe the analysis.

The analysis of a single artifact forms the foundation of decision making, which is discussed in more detail in chapter 4 (page 71). Before setting goals, students need to explore their current state, which is often best done by looking at artifacts first. By examining a sample of learning, students have the opportunity to focus on something tangible, manageable, and immediate. Furthermore, this type of analysis affords students the chance to practice critical self-assessment subskills such as noticing, remembering, and describing. When this type of analysis is structured to ask learners to compare aspects of their work with specific success criteria, it also addresses the subskills of relating, comparing, and connecting.

The following are sample prompts you could use to guide artifact analysis.

- What do you think you did well on this sample? Which aspects of the sample show strength? Which part makes you feel most confident?

- What was challenging about this sample? Why did you find it challenging?

- What did you enjoy the most and the least?

- What strategies did you try? How successful were they? What might you do again next time?

- When did you know you had done a good job? What clues in your sample told you your efforts were successful?

- Does your sample address the success criteria? Offer evidence for each criterion.

- How did you know what was best to focus on in this sample?

- What evidence do you have to support your analysis and reflections?

- Where is the best part of your work? Highlight it. Note what makes it best.
- Where do you think your thinking or ideas were the strongest?
- What was the easiest part of this learning, and what was the hardest part?
- If you could change your answers (ideas, presentation, and so on), what would you add or take out?
- If you had half an hour to improve your work on this sample, what would you focus on? Why?
- Is there another explanation for what happened?
- What supports do you think you still need (for example, people, tools, information, practice, or instruction)?
- What questions do you still have?

Figure 3.1 is a template students can use to analyze a single artifact. Following the students' analyses, next steps for learning should become clear. If this isn't the case, more modeling and instruction may be needed to guide the analysis.

Figure 3.2 (page 52) offers an alternate template students can use to analyze one artifact.

In looking at these two samples, note how clear it becomes what the next steps might be for the students and the teacher. In the first sample, it is clear that the student needs more instruction in the skill of determining multiples. In the second sample, the student is unclear about the qualities of an effective personal response. Clarifying success criteria and modeling the process for creating a personal response would be appropriate. The good news is, in both cases, the students were able to identify their needs. This is the power of student self-analysis.

Reflecting on Strategies and Processes in Relation to Artifacts and Data

Reflecting on strategies and processes in relation to artifacts and data allows students to think about *how* they approach products or performances and the decisions they make. This analysis goes beyond comparing an artifact to success criteria. It requires students to think about *why* they may have ended up with the results they did. Did they approach the task logically? Did they prepare enough? Did they ask the right questions and gather enough evidence? This type of analysis invites learners to explicitly connect their results with their actions and decisions.

Sample Artifact Analysis 1: Reviewing My Results (Grades 4–12)

*Note: This template is most appropriate for artifacts that contain correct or incorrect responses.

Name: Ryder   Date: October 6
Sample: Factors and multiples test   Grade Level: Sixth

Review your sample and mark whether each problem is correct or incorrect. Next, look at the questions that were incorrect and decide whether you made a simple mistake or a larger error. If your mistake was small, mark the Simple Mistake column. For all the remaining incorrect responses, mark the Need Help column. Don't forget to congratulate yourself for your correct responses.

Problem	Learning Target	Correct	Incorrect	Simple Mistake	Need Help
1	Determine factors	X			
2	Determine factors		X	X	
3	Determine multiples		X		X
4	Determine multiples		X		X

FIGURE 3.1: Sample artifact analysis using one artifact—Marking a choice.

Sample Artifact Analysis 2: Reviewing My Assignment (Grades 4–12)

Name: Gabriella   Date: April 6

Sample: Summary and personal response to fiction novel   Grade level: Fifth

> **In your own words, describe what this sample was asking you to do. Include the learning goal or goals, a product or performance description, and all necessary components. Components include table of contents, bibliography, charts, and so on.**

For this sample, I had to do two things: (1) I had to summarize what the first third of the novel was about and remember not to include too much and not too little. I had to describe the main characters and the most important parts of the plot. (2) I needed to offer a personal response to the first part of the novel. This means I had to connect to what I was reading in some way. I had to connect to what was happening, who the characters were, and maybe even where the beginning of the novel took place. Mrs. White reminded us to think about how the characters felt and what motivated their decisions, and try to connect to those things if we could.

> **Describe your process. How did you apply your learning and in what order? What steps did you take? What strategies did you use?**

When I was doing my summary, I kept notes as I read. There were many characters, so I made notes to help me remember the most important things. Mrs. White gave us a chart, which I used for the summary part. I also imagined I was telling someone about the beginning of the book. Thinking about telling instead of writing helped me decide what to say. I also used the chart for the personal response. When I wrote my personal response, I tried to organize it into different parts of the book I connected with and these were my paragraphs.

> **Which parts of this sample went well for you? Which aspects of this sample met the success criteria? Be specific.**

I think my summary was good. I included information about all the main characters and explained how the author set up the events in the book. I think I gave just the right amount of information. For my personal response, I did pretty well. I tried to give evidence from my own life and connect it to the book. There were some things in the book I didn't relate to, and I wasn't sure if I was supposed to work harder at making connections or not. I probably should have asked for help with this, but I ran out of time.

> **Which aspects of this sample need additional time and attention? How do you know? What steps would you take if you had more time?**

Like I said, I think I might not have made enough connections to some parts of the book. For example, I didn't respond to the part of the book when the main character decided to quit her swimming lessons because she was uncomfortable in her swim suit. I need to find out if I am supposed to connect to everything or not when I do a personal response. I will ask Mrs. White for help next time.

FIGURE 3.2: Sample artifact analysis 2—Explaining a choice.

For this type of analysis, it is important for students to have access to documentation (data or artifacts) that reflect learning in progress, as well as success criteria. Photographs or videos are helpful, and so are goal sheets that articulate specific intended actions or steps that students should have taken.

The following are possible prompts to guide strategy or process analysis.

- During this game (performance, lesson, or assessment), when did you make a decision that led you closer to your goal?
- Did you make any decisions that led you away from a goal?
- Did you try something and then try something different? Why?
- How did you know when you should change your approach?
- When were you able to identify the main idea of the text? What process did you use to arrive at your answer?
- How can you tell the difference between interesting and important details?
- What strategies will you use next time you are identifying important details (solving a multi-step problem, designing a prototype, and so on)?

- What strategies did you use to make sure you answered the whole problem? How do you know you did not leave out any important parts?
- Which strategy was most useful for this task (performance or something else)? Why?
- How did you know when a strategy you were using was not working?
- What are your tips and tricks for learning this?
- Is there another explanation for what happened?
- Where might you seek new ways to approach this? Who might have new ideas?
- How might someone else support you? What do you need from your teacher?
- What questions do you still have?

Figure 3.3 offers a completed sample template teachers can use to practice this type of analysis with elementary students, while figure 3.4 (page 54) offers a completed sample template teachers can use with middle and high school students.

The analysis tool in figure 3.3 invites students in elementary classrooms to reflect on their strategies following a specific learning experience. It encourages students to consider whether the strategies they used to learn helped them or not. This tool depends on teachers naming and modeling potential strategies so they become familiar to students.

This is what we were learning today:

We were learning how to make maps and use all the right symbols.

These are the strategies I tried today:

I looked at the example Mr. Gonzales had at the front of the room. I asked my partner for help when I wasn't sure. I used the checklist to make sure I had everything on there.

These strategies worked! I will keep doing these things:

All of them worked because I finished my map. The example was the most helpful because I like looking at examples.

These are things I still need to figure out:

My partner didn't know one answer, so I had to guess. Also, I wasn't sure if we had to color everything really dark. It wasn't on the checklist.

FIGURE 3.3: Sample process analysis for elementary students—My strategies.

*Visit **go.SolutionTree.com/assessment** for a free blank reproducible version of this figure.*

> My strengths by target (correct and confident):
> - Making and finding figures of speech
> - Identifying genres and author's purpose
> - Summarizing
> - Identifying explicit messages
> - Connecting to a text
>
> My highest priority for study (incorrect and challenging):
> - Making inferences
> - Offering evidence for responses from the text (direct citations and paraphrasing)
> - Organizing my responses so they are clear (multi-paragraph)
>
> My highest priority for review or practice (incorrect but simple mistake):
> - Finding evidence from the text (at least two and from different places in the text)
>
> Strategies I plan on using to learn what I need to learn:
> - Making a chart and forcing myself to find enough evidence
> - Practicing direct citation and paraphrasing of the same evidence (two ways)
> - Getting feedback from a partner about the clarity of my answers
> - Highlighting places where I am making an inference

FIGURE 3.4: Sample process analysis for middle and high school students—Planning a review.

*Visit **go.SolutionTree.com/assessment** for a free blank reproducible version of this figure.*

The analysis tool in figure 3.4 invites students in middle and high school to reflect on a larger formative assessment or significant artifact or artifacts and make decisions about preparing for a summative assessment. It asks students to acknowledge strengths (areas where studying may not be necessary) and also differentiate between study and review or practice.

Analyzing the Relationship Between Two Artifacts

Connecting ideas between multiple artifacts helps students compare their approaches to learning when artifacts represent similar learning goals in different ways (for example, varied writing samples about different topics with a shared goal of effective organization; different mathematics problems that capture the skill of adding fractions) and when different learning goals are demonstrated using a similar process (for example, two maps with one showing population density and another showing geographical features; multiple speech videos sharing arguments on a variety of topics). As long as something is similar between artifacts (the same learning goals or the same methods or processes of demonstrating learning), then students can make comparisons and gain insights from analysis and reflection. Comparing two artifacts allows students to see self-assessment as more than just reflecting on a particular product at a particular moment in time. Instead, they can see that learning is iterative and develops from one task to the next. They discover how the development of skills and knowledge serves not only the current learning experience but future learning experiences as well.

For this type of analysis, students need two or more artifacts that allow them to make comparisons in relation to both success criteria as well as to strategies applied and decisions made. These artifacts can include assessments, practice assignments, drafts, and revised copies of work, videos, photographs, checklists, or any other documentation that reflects thinking and learning. It is also important for students to be clear about the learning goals for each sample and have the success criteria in front of them and easily understood (co-constructed is a great option here).

Providing prompts during this type of analysis is critical in helping students analyze specific relationships between two or more artifacts. As always, teachers need to be clear about what they are hoping to achieve through this kind of analysis. It may be helpful to consider the following questions.

- Do you want students to analyze the degree to which each artifact addresses specific *success criteria*? For example, you may ask students to compare the degree to which their artifacts reflect the skill of writing a compelling introduction or designing an informational text that communicates a message through the use of images.
- Do you want students to consider the *success of strategies* they applied during artifact creation? For example, you may ask learners to reflect on the two brainstorming strategies they applied and decide which one served them best.
- Do you want students to use the artifacts to reflect on their decisions relating to the *contexts they established* while creating the artifacts? For example, you may ask them to reflect on whether the decision to work alone or work with a partner served them best or whether their decision to write while listening to music was a good one, based on evidence from their artifacts (one written with music and one written without).

The following are sample prompts to guide the analysis of the relationship between two or more artifacts.

- Compare your responses this time to last time. How have they improved? What changed?
- Which strategies helped you approach this task with confidence? Which strategies did you use in both samples? How did you know which strategy to use?
- What is something new you tried in the later sample as compared to the first sample? What approach did you try differently the second time around?
- Did your prediction (solution, approach, introduction, tactic, and so on) ever change? Why?
- What do you want to remember about approaching a task, response, and so on, like this?
- Which sample shows the greatest strength in the area of (insert success criterion)? Why?
- Which sample shows the greatest difficulty with (insert success criterion)? Why?
- How did you ready yourself for success with each sample? Did one approach give you better results? Why do you think that is?
- Which sample best reflects your point of view (your most creative ideas, your most organized thoughts, and so on)? How do you know? Underline the part of the sample that does the best job.
- Which decisions did you make that you wish you could change? Which decisions did you make in the first sample that you changed in the second?
- Which sample was harder to do? Why?
- Which sample do you feel is the better example of you, your confidence, or your independence?
- Which sample are you most proud of and why?
- Which targets were the most difficult to master? Why do you think that was?
- How might someone else support you? What do you need from your teacher?
- What questions do you still have?
- Is there another explanation for what happened?

Figure 3.5 (page 56) offers a template to help students compare multiple artifacts.

Analyzing Data

To analyze data, students will need access to data. These data can reflect quantitative judgments (formative or summative scores or grades) or qualitative decisions (rubric levels). There need to be enough data present for students to organize them appropriately (in tables, charts, or graphs) and then analyze patterns, relationships, and anomalies. Teachers can provide these data to the students or, even better, students can generate these data and also organize, graph, or record

STUDENT SELF-ASSESSMENT

Name: _____ Date: _____

Sample: _____

Students may find this tool useful when exploring more than one sample in their data notebooks or portfolios. Using this tool, students compare either different versions of the same product or completely separate samples that reflect similar goals. When the samples are set side by side, this tool invites students to think about what the samples tell them about decisions they made, goals they are exploring, and questions that remain.

Sample description:	Sample description:
My goals for this sample were:	**My goals for this sample were:**
What I learned:	**What I learned:**

When I look at both samples, I can see:

I still wonder:

This makes me think I might:

FIGURE 3.5: Tool for comparing more than one artifact.

*Visit **go.SolutionTree.com/assessment** for a free reproducible version of this figure.*

them so they can readily recognize key information and make decisions based on what they see.

As stated earlier, data may reflect smaller targets within larger learning goals. For example, students may graph their reading fluency as part of the broader goal of reading and comprehending grade-level texts. In this case, it would be important that students understand how reading fluency contributes to overall comprehension and enjoyment while reading. Otherwise, tracking fluency numbers becomes an end in and of itself, which minimizes the role fluency plays in more complex goals. Furthermore, the moment student reading fluency reflects consistent proficiency, these data need to shift to another aspect of reading comprehension (such as reading expression or making connections).

The decision to track growth in relation to smaller targets is fine as long as these smaller targets always connect back to the larger goals of learning. It is helpful for students to understand the role of short-term goals in achieving long-term growth. For example, tracking the number of correct spelling words in isolation (as generated from spelling tests) without ever reflecting on strategies for spelling correctly or without reinforcing the need for students to apply correct spelling within their daily writing, is collecting data without advancing learning. This example illustrates a disconnect between short-term goals (spell these ten words correctly) and a longer-term purpose of enhancing strategies for spelling and overall written communication. When the data collection process gets stuck and does not reflect students' current needs or long-term goals, data notebooks and other self-assessment tools become a chore and do not demonstrate authentic growth.

In addition to monitoring and celebrating both short- and long-term growth, engaging students in data provides learners the opportunity to practice specific data organization and analysis skills. Certainly, these skills are reflected in specific learning goals at the elementary, middle, and high school levels (in mathematics and science courses, for example), but even the youngest students can begin to recognize patterns in simple graphs and relate symbols to values. Bar graphs and pie charts are great tools for showing early elementary students the relationships between learning in classrooms and ways to represent this learning visually.

In the beginning, monitoring students as they engage in this work will be important, but as students grow older and build confidence and skill, this analysis can increasingly become the students' own responsibility. Ultimately, we want students to clearly understand the role data have in driving learning forward. No matter what we track, we want learners to see assessment information as something that is future focused. This is why a focus on formative data is preferable, so students can experience action in response to what they see in their own data.

The following are sample prompts to guide the analysis of quantitative and qualitative data (remember to select only a few from this list for each analysis).

- How do these data make you feel as a learner?
- What surprises you about these data?
- What does not surprise you about these data?
- In what ways do these data not represent you? In what ways do they represent you?
- What does your data show from one effort to the next? What patterns are you noticing?
- Where do you see strength? What parts of your data make you feel most confident?
- What does your data tell you about how you are doing on the goal of (insert target or goal)?
- Complete the following statement: "I used to . . . , but now I . . . ."
- What was the easiest part of this learning? The hardest part?
- What is something you have been working on that is clearly shown in your data?
- Does your data show improvement? Where? Why do you think this growth occurred?
- Where do these data indicate challenge? Why was this challenging? Were you able to find a solution to the challenges you were experiencing?
- Is there something these data do not show but you think is important?
- Which targets have you found most useful to learn? Why?
- What do you think these data explain? Why?
- What evidence have you gathered to support your claims?

- What claims can you make from your evidence?
- Is there another explanation for what happened?
- How do your data connect to decisions you made, things that happened, or both?
- What might you do to improve these data? What might you do differently next time?
- Do your data indicate that you are proficient in one goal so you can move on to another? Explain your thinking.
- Imagine next time you look at your data that you see evidence of growth. What would have happened between now and then?
- How might someone else support you? What do you need from your teacher?
- What questions do you still have?

Figure 3.6 shows sample data sets and prompts to illustrate this option for analysis.

Documenting Data in Various Ways

The following are additional ways to engage students in documentation (data or artifacts) analysis. Using a variety of approaches can increase learners' confidence with the overall skill of analysis and also can increase the likelihood that certain approaches improve access for learners who vary in preferences and skills and are working on different short-term goals.

- Use colored highlighters to signal different degrees of proficiency or different examples of success criteria within work or data. For example: *In your persuasive writing, highlight sentences that most strongly reflect your thesis in green, and those that partially reflect it in yellow.* For many students (excepting those with visual challenges), color is a quick way to help identify patterns and trends, as well as specific strengths and needs. An alternative is to annotate artifacts, data, or both with symbols that represent key features. For example: *Place a star anywhere in your solution where you are unsure of your chosen strategy. Place a checkmark next to any part of your solution where you are confident in your approach.*

- Create templates that invite multiple people into the analysis process. For example, it may be helpful to pair a data set or an artifact with a chart that lists essential learning targets and then provide a column for student reflection and a column for teacher reflection. Finally, you could include space for students to respond to both reflections (both yours and theirs) and make decisions.

- Include sample data sets and artifact analyses for students to refer to when building independence. Sometimes, one example is worth many sets of instructions. Another option is to model the process and have students work in pairs to create a list of instructions based on the model.

- When students are taking an assessment that contains selected-response questions, have them indicate the degree of confidence in their responses by shading the letter solidly if they are sure of their choice or simply marking their selection with an *X* if they are unsure. This helps with deeper analysis after scoring the assessment. Follow-up questions or graphing could explore not only the number correct but also the number for which the student was confident.

You may want to consider discussing the concept of *false confidence* with students—a belief that proficiency exists when more growth is, in fact, needed. For example, a student might believe that their response to a question is correct or robust when there are actually key components missing or when their solution is inaccurate. Recognizing false confidence is important in moving toward proficiency. I sometimes call this phenomenon *coming to understand what I don't know*, and it is an important first step in rich learning. As students begin to see that they have more to learn, they then open up to ideas that might kick-start the process. Learning about false confidence as a real and even normal concept in places where learning is happening is important for disrupting misconceptions and connecting confidence to accuracy. You know learning has moved from surface to deep when students know and can perform critical skills, have confidence that they can learn, *and* know when their confidence is accurate.

Engaging in Analysis and Reflection   59

	Main Idea	Key Details
September 6		
September 20		
October 4		
October 15		
November 1		
December 12		

Key

	Building Readiness
	Exploring and Practicing
	Independently Proficient
	Extending and Enriching

- What do you think these data explain?
- Where do these data indicate strength?
- Where do these data indicate challenge?
- Does your data show that you need to move on to another goal? How do you know?

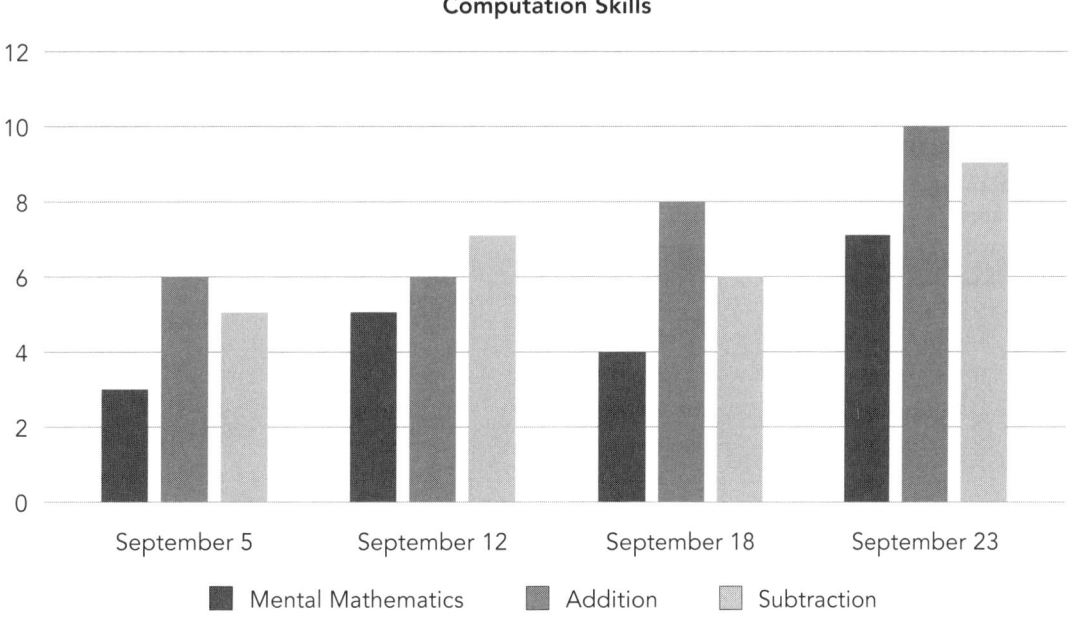

- Where do the data indicate strength?
- Where do the data indicate challenge?
- Imagine next time you look at your data that you see evidence of growth. What would have happened between now and then?

FIGURE 3.6: Sample data sets and prompts.

- For students who are ready for more sophisticated analysis, consider inviting them to explore the connections between multiple data sets. For example, they might look at their data for accuracy in mathematics computation and relate it to their data for speed. Or they might connect their accuracy in reading to their accuracy in mathematics. They can then begin to explore whether taking a little more time increases or decreases their accuracy or whether they have more accuracy in one area of learning over another and why. This kind of analysis leads to a richer exploration of learning and how learning skills connect to each other.

- Consider using a two-column approach to analysis. Column 1 asks students to notice and describe what they see (Here's What I Notice), and column 2 asks them to reflect and comment on what they see (What This Means . . .).

- Have students keep a running list of strategies that have led them toward success and strategies that have led them away from success. This can encourage learners to develop a sense of how they learn best. It also can invite reflection on strategies that are universally useful and those that work best for specific people in specific contexts. This record of strategies could be divided into *observable strategies* and *in-the-head strategies*. Often, students are under the false impression that people who are proficient do not use strategies. It's important to clarify that *all* strong learners apply strategies—you just can't always see them. This exercise can help build this understanding.

Where to Start

Sometimes, when exploring a complex process like analysis, it is helpful to focus on the very first steps we might take to begin. While the following four steps are not comprehensive, they are a way to begin this process if you are looking for a starting point.

1. **Model analysis for students using a single artifact or data point:** Relate elements of the artifact or data to success criteria. Be explicit in showing what data can tell us about quality and strategy use (and also what it can't tell us). Model how an artifact or data in combination with success criteria can help us with next steps.

2. **Select a prompt that inspires analysis and invite students to reflect on a work sample in progress:** Talk with students about their experience with reflecting. Was it easy? Was it challenging? Why? Help them see the importance of pausing and looking back before moving ahead.

3. **Have students practice comparing a first draft or performance with a revision or a second attempt:** Talk about the choices they made that were different in the first and second iteration and why they decided to keep some aspects of their work from one sample to the next. Talk explicitly about strategies they used to arrive at both samples.

4. **Use a simple data-analysis protocol to look at a data set:** Be sure to draw their attention to strengths and areas requiring growth. Make sure students see the connections between their analysis and the evidence in front of them.

TOOLS TO SUPPORT SELF-ASSESSMENT

The following templates and tools can provide a framework for inviting students into data and artifact analysis and reflection. Some are more appropriate for students in early elementary (grades K–3), and others are better suited to upper elementary, middle school, or high school students.

➤ **"Margin Symbols" reproducible (page 62):** This tool invites students in grades 4–12 to annotate their own documentation (for example, test, assignment, essay, or concept map) as a way of deciding which aspects hold strength and which could use some additional instruction and practice.

➤ **"Reflection on a Work Sample: Single-Point Rubric" reproducible (page 63):** This tool invites students in grades 4–12 to reflect on success criteria in relation to their own sample and make decisions about next steps.

➤ **"Tracking My Progress" reproducible (page 64):** This tool invites students in all grade levels (with guidance in early elementary) to identify key learning goals within a unit and use simple symbols to track learning as the unit unfolds. You may want to work through the first sections of the tool (unit title, big idea, and targets of topics) with students. As the unit progresses, students can spend short periods of time reflecting on their progress, using the symbols in the key. Based on their reflections, you can make subsequent instructional decisions.

➢ **"Growth Card" reproducible (page 65):** This tool invites students at any grade level to reflect on a change in any aspect of their learning. For example, a student in physical education might say, "I used to wait at the net for the puck, and now I move around the offensive zone, trying to pass to anyone who is open."

➢ **"Reflecting on Success Criteria" reproducible (page 66):** This tool invites students in grades 4–12 to identify success criteria for a product or performance and reflect several times on their progress in relation to the criteria. Students can use this tool to identify questions and challenges as they occur. Students can use it to outline the success criteria for a specific product or performance (either given to them or co-constructed with them) and then reflect, multiple times, on their own progress in relation to the criteria. Teachers can work with students to ensure their questions are answered and progress is occurring.

➢ **"Most Important Things" reproducible (page 67):** This tool invites students at any grade level to reflect on what they learned during a class period, an entire day, or even a week, and identify the most important things they learned. Students can then turn to their data notebooks or portfolios and identify samples that represent strength, need, and challenge.

➢ **"My Action Plan" reproducible (page 68):** This tool invites students at any grade level to reflect on a specific challenge they are experiencing and begin to imagine solutions to the challenge.

➢ **"Assess and Reflect on Reading Skills" reproducible (page 69):** This tool invites students in grades K–6 to reflect on reading comprehension strategies following the completion of a comprehension task. You could adapt it for any subject area and include the related learning strategies.

QUESTIONS TO GUIDE CONVERSATION AND REFLECTION

On your own or as a part of a collaborative team, consider and discuss the following eight reflective questions.

1. How often do students reflect on incomplete or unrefined artifacts? How often do students receive instruction and time for comparing these kinds of samples to success criteria?

2. Do students collect and organize any form of personal data in relation to skills they are developing? If so, how are students currently using these data? Are they invited to analyze their own data?

3. How often do students reflect on their decision making in relation to products or performances? To what degree do students have the ability to make decisions while at school?

4. How comfortable are learners with being less than proficient? What is their understanding of this occurrence in education?

5. How often do I encourage students to offer their perceptions, understanding, and analysis of what is happening in their daily education?

6. What skills do students need to develop and practice in order to be able to analyze their artifacts and data in a purposeful manner? Where might students hold strength at this point in time? Where might they need support?

7. How are artifact and data analyses different for students than they are for teachers? How are they the same?

8. How might I invite students to analyze their artifacts and data in developmentally appropriate ways? What should I consider when teaching this to specific age groups?

Margin Symbols

Name: _____ Date: _____

Examine a sample from your portfolio. Look at each part of the sample and use the margin symbols to idenfiy those parts that were easy, those that were hard, those that you feel confident doing, and those that you may need more time to learn and pratice. You will use these symbols to help you set goals.

!   This is too hard.

✓   I found this easy or I understand this.

★   I could teach this to someone else.

{ }   Working with a partner might help me more.

+   I need more time with this.

→   I could use some more practice.

Reflection on a Work Sample: Single-Point Rubric

Name: _____ Date: _____

Use the success criteria in the middle column to reflect on your work sample. Consider each criterion and the degree to which it is present in your own work. Offer evidence from your sample to support your ideas. Once you have completed your reflection, submit both your sample and this template to your teacher, who will offer feedback. Then you can use the feedback and your own reflections to make some decisions using the questions at the end of this template.

Student Reflection	Success Criteria	Teacher Feedback

Based on my reflection and teacher feedback, I am going to return to my work and revise the following things:

Date for completion of revisions and resubmission: _____

Student Self-Assessment © 2022 Solution Tree Press • SolutionTree.com
Visit **go.SolutionTree.com/assessment** to download this page.

Tracking My Progress

Name: _____ Date: _____

Work with your teacher to complete the unit title, big idea, and targets or topics. Then reflect on your progress using the symbols in the key.

New unit:		
The big idea for this unit:		
Targets or Topics We Will Explore	**Tracking My Progress**	**Date**

Key:

- ✓ I'm doing just fine.
- → I'm on my way but not quite there yet.
- ? I am sure I need more information or practice.
- * I enjoyed this target or topic.

Growth Card

Name: _____ Date: _____

Think about your learning in the past few days. What is a skill or an understanding you have developed? Think about what you used to know or do that you now understand or can do differently.

I used to:

And now I:

What I am learning:

Reflecting on Success Criteria

Name: _____ Date: _____

Use this tool to outline the success criteria for a specific product or performance, and then reflect on your progress in relation to the criteria.

Criteria for Proficiency	There	Not Yet	Questions I Have

Student Self-Assessment © 2022 Solution Tree Press • SolutionTree.com
Visit **go.SolutionTree.com/assessment** to download this page.

Most Important Things

Name: _____ Date: _____

Use this tool to reflect on what you learned during one class period, during an entire day, or even during a week, and select the most important things you learned. You can then use your data notebook or portfolio to identify samples that represent strength, need, and challenge.

The three most important things we explored and practiced are:

1.

2.

3.

Thinking About My Learning

Using sticky notes, look through your data notebook or portfolio and choose the following samples. On each sticky note, write the category and answer the prompt.

- A sample or data set you would like to do over again. How would you change it if you could?
- A sample or data set that shows growth. How can you provide evidence of this growth?
- A sample or data set that had some hard parts and some easy parts. Which parts were which? How did you deal with the hard parts?

Student Self-Assessment © 2022 Solution Tree Press • SolutionTree.com
Visit **go.SolutionTree.com/assessment** to download this page.

My Action Plan

Name: _____ Date: _____

Sometimes, the things you find difficult offer you the best ideas for growth. Think about your learning today and reflect on the following questions.

Identify Tough Stuff

Something that was tough for me today:

This was really hard for me because:

Next time, I plan to:

Assess and Reflect on Reading Skills

Name: _____ Date: _____

Look at your answers and think of the skills you have that helped you comprehend what you read. Then think of skills you can improve to assist your comprehension of what you read.

Look in the reading skills box below and do the following:
- Shade three skills green that you feel are strengths.
- Shade two skills red that you feel are weaknesses.
- Write one skill you will remember to use the next time you read.

Using pictures	Using titles	Talking to a partner
Decoding (word skills)	Thinking about prior knowledge	Rereading
Asking questions	Listening to someone read	Predicting
Inferencing	Making pictures in my mind	Taking notes as I read

The next time I read, I will remember to:

I will know I am getting better when I:

CHAPTER 4

Imagining Possibilities and Setting Goals

But until a person can say deeply and honestly, "I am what I am today because of the choices I made yesterday," that person cannot say, "I choose otherwise."
—Stephen R. Covey

"Please place your goal cards in front of you and find a pen," the teacher instructs. "You will also need your criteria checklists." She waits for students to get themselves organized. The students pull their goal cards and criteria checklists from envelopes taped to the sides of their desks. "I would like you to work with your accountability partners today. You are going to collaborate to set your goals for our next inquiry experiment." She gives the students a moment to glance at their predetermined partners.

Students have been working on their states of matter unit and are moving into their third experiment. They are very excited about the labs, with participation indicating deep interest. However, when it comes to documenting findings and drawing thoughtful conclusions, the results are less proficient. Students are happy to engage in hands-on learning, but making time to write observations and organize data seems more difficult for many of them.

The teacher asks students to record their rubric scores based on various critical skills in a table in their data notebooks. They keep track of their progress on generating inquiry questions, crafting a strong hypothesis, documenting the experiment procedure, and recording materials, and students show real strength in these areas. They also document their rubric scores in relation to observations, data gathering and analysis, and drawing conclusions. As a class, these results are not as strong.

The teacher decides to invite learners to spend time analyzing their rubric data and reflecting on next steps. "I would like you and your partner to look at your rubric data for the last two experiments and identify the skills for which you are already proficient and those for which you still need practice. I would like you to record strengths and needs in a T-chart in your data notebook. Make sure you assign the T-chart a date, so when we check back after this experiment, you can chart your improvement."

The teacher turns to the whiteboard and draws the T-chart she wants students to replicate in their notebooks. She lists the key skills underneath and models how to decide in which column of the T-chart to place each skill. After opening the floor to questions, students find their accountability partners and begin to analyze their rubric data and create their T-charts.

After ten minutes, students seem to be finishing this analysis, so the teacher continues with the next step. "I would now like you and your partner to have a conversation about the skills you placed in the Needs Practice column. Select one to two skills and write them on your goal card, along with the date. If you don't have any skills needing improvement, please raise your hand." The teacher makes a note of the two students with whom she needs to work on an extension goal and asks them to remain with their partner for support. She reassures them that she will visit them after this next step.

"If your accountability partner has a skill in the Needs Practice column and that same skill is in your Strength column, could you spend a few minutes showing them your last lab write-up and helping with strategies for strengthening these skills? Take turns building up each other's strategies." With a student volunteer, the teacher demonstrates a possible conversation that might occur.

"On your goal card, record the strategies you learn underneath the skill so you remember to try them when we do this next experiment," she instructs. "If you both have a skill in the Needs Practice column, you will get a chance to find someone in the room who might be able to offer you support."

When students begin to engage in their support sessions, the teacher visits the two students needing extension and discusses a new way to record observations and organize data. She asks them to list data organization and analysis extension as the goal skills on their goal cards.

The class finishes their goal session with students finding other classmates who show strength with the skills they choose to improve. The teacher circulates around the room and listens to conversations, making sure the strategies shared are helpful and specific. She finds herself adding strategies on only a couple of occasions, when a larger group of learners needs extra support. Once everyone has at least two strategies to apply to each goal in the next experiment and write-up, the class is ready to begin the inquiry session.

RESPOND TO THE SCENARIO

Answer the following questions using information from the preceding scenario.
- How did the learners use their data as a catalyst for establishing goals?
- Who was making the decisions? What decisions were they making?
- How did students arrive at strategies for growth? What was the role of the teacher?

There is something powerful about a personal goal. It reflects optimism for the future, certainly, but it also speaks of a desire to change something about ourselves and, most importantly, it speaks of owning that change and understanding we are in charge. Setting goals requires true efficacy and agency and, to be honest, this isn't always easy to achieve authentically in a school setting where many decisions are already made for teachers and students. There are prescribed learning goals and curricula, mandated schedules and bells, specific resources and learning platforms, and a structure that often places decision making in the hands of someone other than the learners. However, the importance of personal goal setting for students is well documented in the research (Black & Wiliam, 1998; Burns, Martin, & Collie, 2018; Gregory et al., 2011; Hattie & Donoghue, 2016; OECD, 2017; Ross, 2006), and it not only serves academic ends, but social-emotional ones as well.

So how do you teach and support students in the skill of goal setting? Like most aspects of education, it starts with relationships. Usually, good relationships are based on a shared belief in each other. In a strong relationship, both people change to address contexts as they emerge. For example, in a friendship, both people involved may change and adapt to ensure their friend's needs for frequency of contact, clarity of communication, or shared interests are being met, even when life's circumstances present new and shifting needs. We trust that we can both imagine a future that looks a little different from the current state because we will both, inevitably, have the need to change. This is the nature of caring and relationships in a world where things are rarely static.

The same holds true in an education context where relationships are foundational. Self-assessment and goal setting call on a partnership between teachers and learners, where decisions are shared and outcomes, successful or not, are experienced together. Teachers and learners must have a belief in each other to shift and adapt to contexts, with the best interests of both learning and the learner in mind. This reflective and responsive stance is part of a classroom culture that embraces and supports healthy goal setting by students.

Whether we are using data notebooks, portfolios, or other self-assessment tools, intentionally making time and providing resources to examine the current state of learning and think about a future state that reflects optimal growth is vital, as is supporting the development of goal-setting and action-planning skills *as well as* communicating to students that we recognize the important role they play in education. By inviting students to set their own goals, we are building independence, decision making, and investment in the learning experiences we so carefully consider in our daily planning. We are also communicating a belief in students as agents of change and as important people in the learning relationship. This is a powerful message for students.

In this chapter, you will learn several considerations for self-assessment related to imagination and goal setting, including the importance of timing and setting short- and long-term goals. You also will learn effective strategies, such as establishing predictable routines and reinforcing the significance of student ownership in setting goals for learning. At the end of the chapter, you will find practical templates and tools to help you and your students engage in goal setting, along with steps for where to start and questions for conversation and reflection with colleagues and students.

Elements of Goal Setting

While this chapter offers practical tools and templates to support goal setting in education contexts, the discussion on this topic must begin with the elements of imagination, hope, resilience, and inspiration. Without these things, goal setting cannot live up to its potential to facilitate growth and achievement. Each of these elements moves students toward authentic efficacy in personal decision making.

Imagination

Chapter 3 (page 45) discusses the self-assessment subskills. Within that list is a key skill that impacts goal setting: *imagining*. Educators and curricular standards often overlook the importance of imagination, but without it, students can't explore beyond their current reality when setting future goals. The Centre for Imagination in Research, Culture, and Education (n.d.) describes imagination this way:

> It is the ability to think of the possible, not just the actual; it is the source of invention, novelty, and flexibility in human thinking; it is not distinct from rationality but is rather a capacity that greatly enriches rational thinking; it is tied to our ability to form images in the mind, and image-forming commonly involves emotion.

The role of imagination in manifesting a future state different from the current state (the foundation of goal setting) is shared by researcher and professor Maxine Greene (2000), who states, "Of all our cognitive capacities, imagination is the one that permits us to give credence to alternative realities. It allows us to break with the taken for granted, to set aside familiar definitions and distinctions" (p. 3). She goes on to clarify, "It takes imagination on the part of the young people to perceive openings through which they can move" (p. 14). In other words, students have to create possibility and design actions that will move them into that possibility. Greene goes on to articulate the bridge between the past and the future: "To learn and to teach, one must have an awareness of leaving something behind while reaching toward something new, and this kind of awareness must be linked to imagination" (p. 20). Imagination drives the new. It creates space in the learning process to move in new directions.

Without imagination, it is very challenging for students to see that their current learning status could be any different. Without imagination, students might struggle to know how to change when we ask them to make different decisions or take different actions. This is why exercising imagination is so critical for the skill of goal setting. When we teach students how to imagine, we help them become comfortable with seeing their learning in new ways.

When we ask students to select a short-term goal to focus on, we are asking them to imagine a new outcome. When we invite them to design actions that may get them closer to their goal (or goals), we are asking them to imagine ways to make decisions and choices. When we make time for students to reflect on their decisions and determine the degree to which their goals were met, we are asking them to reflect on the relationship between their imaginations when they were setting intentions and their current state, when the imagined actions are enacted. Imagination and goal setting are inextricably linked and so developing the skill of imagination is critical in today's classrooms, when self-assessment is the desired outcome.

Hope and Resilience

In a goal-setting context, imagination has a strong relationship with hope. When we imagine ways to achieve our goals, we are hopeful that those ways will yield results. This position of hope is critical in sustaining confidence, risk taking, and overall optimism. The process of setting goals, designing actions, and then periodically reflecting on the goals is critical for building a healthy relationship between imagination and hope at the front end, and risk taking and critical analysis after actions have been taken.

In *Poor Students, Rich Teaching*, Eric Jensen (2019) emphasizes the importance of building hope as "a constant process of instilling a lifelong sense of possibility for something good" (p. 83). Related to goal setting specifically, he states: "Managing your destiny is a hope builder. . . . Teach students how to assess progress, get feedback, and correct their courses in order to score [improve]. . . . Students need to see that they are improving and getting closer to their goals" (pp. 83–84).

As stated earlier, it is important for students to develop resilience to face the likelihood that some actions they may have imagined will *not* actually get them closer to their goals. This is the heart of building strong learners—learners who recognize that imagination and goal setting are what keep us focused on the future, but failure and setbacks also are part of that forward movement. It is challenging, as a teacher, to face moments when students realize that despite their desire to reach a goal and even despite their efforts, they still have come up short. It is natural to want to step in and fix the problem so students remain hopeful and cooperative, but this overcompensation, in fact, teaches students that when they fail in school, someone will solve their problems for them. It may even communicate that they are not capable of solving their own problems. Teaching is more complex than this, because we want students to make the right decisions, but we also want them to work through setbacks on their own so they develop multiple critical skills (academic and social-emotional) at the same time.

In "Productive Struggle Is a Learner's Sweet Spot," Barbara Blackburn (2018) claims that providing an environment that sets high expectations and scaffolding without offering excessive help to students is key to *productive struggle*. She states:

> Productive struggle is what I call the "sweet spot" in between scaffolding and support. Rather than immediately helping students at the first sign of trouble, we should allow them to work through struggles independently before we offer assistance. That may sound counterintuitive, since many of us assume that helping students learn means protecting them from negative feelings of frustration. But for students to become independent learners, they must learn to persist in the face of challenge.

This is the potential of strong goal-setting processes. We can invite future-focused planning to make time for reflection and adjustment. We can support students in imagining different outcomes and ways to get at them, but goal setting allows students to remain in control of both decisions and the consequences of those decisions. This is powerful agency, and it nurtures a relationship between teachers and students that is supportive and reflective while still allowing for the complexity that true deep learning requires.

Inspirational Tools

One way to guide students to imagine different decisions and outcomes without stepping in to make the changes for them is to engage them in *exemplars*, *varied samples*, and *mentor texts*.

- **Exemplars** are examples of excellence in a task (often created by learners who are representative of students we are teaching). In a 2002 study by researchers Paul Orsmond, Stephen Merry, and Kevin Reiling, self- and peer assessment were implemented, leveraging the use of exemplars. The study showed that exemplars can help students develop a greater understanding of success criteria as well as the subject goals themselves. Exemplars also supported higher levels of achievement and the formation of constructive feedback. When students explore exemplars and consider the attributes that make a quality product or performance, they enhance their own potential to replicate the same level of quality in their own work.

- **Samples** can include examples of work not yet refined and can emerge from works in progress within the classroom or from samples collected or generated in previous years with other groups of learners (with permission). Teachers may even create their own samples to model strategies for improving or enhancing the sample. As Hilary Seitz (2008) explains in her article "The Power of Documentation in the Early Childhood Classroom," samples can offer a springboard for the next iteration of learning: "The children and teacher revisit the encounter [learning experience] through the documentation and reflect on the experience, which helps the children continue their conversation and drives forward their interest" (p. 91). Imperfect samples generate analysis and invite learners to strategize ways to move closer to quality products and performances.

- **Mentor texts** are texts, often written by experts (authors, researchers, scientists, and so on), which teachers and students can return to repeatedly for many different purposes. By using examples of both proficient and not-yet-proficient products and performances, we can structure conversations about success criteria, model processes and strategies for creating and refining products, and demonstrate the evolution of learning over time. For example, some people use mentor texts to model ways professional writers capture readers' attention, communicate for a specific purpose, and craft ideas in innovative ways. Similarly, in science classes, inviting students to explore scientific articles and formats for experimentation can assist learners in understanding the complexity of scientific inquiry.

By combining the use of exemplars, samples, and mentor texts with goal setting, we can structure ways for students to more easily imagine different outcomes and plan to take actions that will shift their future state. This approach can ignite curiosity and interest and support students enough to guide them to greater success without making every decision for them.

Building goal setting into lessons and units can nurture independence, agency, and problem solving. It can support the development of imagination and hope while making space for failure and revision. It allows teachers to guide students in the quest for growth without over-stepping and usurping control. Finally, it supports a relationship between teachers and students that is grounded in a deep belief in students' capabilities to control aspects of their school experiences. It is a key part of a classroom culture that strives for authentic partnership, trust, and inquiry.

Considerations for Self-Assessment

Goal setting is the *action* portion of self-assessment, the part of the process that invites decision making, planning, and forward momentum. After students document their thinking and skill development and engage in documentation analysis to highlight strengths and needs, it's time to plan for next steps. Some of these next steps will simply be a continuation of effective strategies and approaches, while others require a change in direction. When students set goals, they are asking themselves, "What is working for me in my pursuit of specific goals? What is challenging me? What do I need to do moving forward? What supports would help me right now?"

In order for goal setting to be effective and truly actionable, you must take things into consideration. The timing of goal setting must be right and explicitly connect short-term efforts to long-term outcomes. The goals must hold specific characteristics and students must maintain ownership as much as possible. I explore these considerations more fully in the following section.

Timing

The timing of goal setting is critical for both its success in improving academic goals and for its role in creating and sustaining hope and a belief that it actually serves a purpose. Many educators are familiar with the popular SMART goal format (Conzemius & O'Neill, 2014; Doran, 1981)—specific, measurable, achievable, realistic, and timebound. SMART goals have guided goal setting in many facets of educational planning, from the system to the classroom level. Timing is a key feature of this widely accepted strategy, because when students decide to implement goals and reflect on progress, this impacts the speed and accuracy with which they are able to advance toward their intended outcomes.

Students will very quickly become disenfranchised in goal setting if it is simply added on to the end of a unit plan or sits outside actual decision making and lesson planning. Students have to experience the impact of their decisions immediately. Goal setting works best when it occurs *before* we create products and enact performances. Teachers also must make time *while* practicing, drafting, and exploring for students to reflect on the trajectory of their decisions, so they can work with students to make adjustments as needed. Researcher Chase Nordengren (2019) calls these frequent goal setting moments *check ins*, and he asserts, "These check ins allow for frequent revision of goals based on student progress, preventing students from feeling discouraged. With several opportunities to observe progress, a goal not yet met becomes a goal that can be met in the future with additional effort."

Teachers also have to expose students to success criteria early in the learning process. How and precisely when teachers share these criteria are flexible and depend on the kind of learning being explored, but without criteria, students are unclear about what they are trying to achieve. Dimich (2015) explains, "In the absence of a clear idea of the criteria for quality work or learning goals, students set superficial goals" (p. 98). Imagine trying to set a goal related to parking a car if you had never seen an example of proficient parking, never watched someone park, and no one clarified expectations before taking your driving exam. Co-constructing criteria, modeling the process for arriving at quality learning, and sharing exemplars are all important parts of setting students up for successful goal setting.

The processes of setting goals and establishing success criteria are not without nuance. In my book *Unlocked: Assessment as the Key to Everyday Creativity in the Classroom* (White, 2019), I share the notion that the timing for establishing success criteria may change, depending on the learning experience. When we invite students to engage in creative processes, for example, a slight delay in establishing criteria might be optimal. There are times when we want students to freely engage in exploration, which involves manipulating materials, generating questions, and engaging in compelling, unstructured learning contexts. In this case, generating success criteria too early might limit the level of inquiry in which students are encouraged to engage. For example, if you invite students to create a new game in physical education, you might delay communicating success criteria until students have a chance to explore potential equipment, the space in which the game will be played, and their own imaginative ideas for the end goal of the game. This delay prevents students from "over-filtering" their initial ideas and reducing their creative capacities. Once this exploratory work is done, initial goals and success criteria will serve as the catalyst for the next stage of the creative process: elaboration.

By contrast, in learning contexts where students are very unfamiliar with a particular process or product (as presented in a learning goal), it may be advantageous to introduce success criteria and exemplars immediately. This allows students to visualize their own efforts in tangible ways and see the path to success more clearly. For example, if the goal of *formally analyzing an image* is brand new to learners, we may want to clarify the need to delay opinions and look at individual elements, such as line, value, color, and texture first. Then, when analyzing the image, students can describe how these elements relate to each other and their interpretation of the image. Further, students can support their analyses with specific examples from the image itself as well as any research they may have done. If this is not a process students have experienced before, by explaining the qualities of a strong analysis we are helping them engage in the image more fully from the outset. If the goal seems too far away, it is difficult to know which first steps to take.

Understanding learning goals and where students are in their own learning journeys can help us decide when it makes the most sense to be explicit in describing quality and when it makes sense to step back a little and let students lead the way. If we ask students to set a learning goal and they seem challenged with making the goal realistic, practical, and connected to the experience at hand, then we may need to offer more tangible guidance. On the other hand, if student goals seem uninspired and rigid, it may signal a need to invite more open-ended exploration before narrowing our focus. This is how goal setting can move learning forward while also providing teachers valuable information about where students are in their journey. When processes are not working well, it tells us we need to do things differently somehow. This is the give and take of all assessment processes—feedback goes in two directions.

Short- and Long-Term Goals

When I think about the goals I set for myself in daily life, I know some of them are short-term goals ("I will go for a long walk today," or "I will write for an hour this morning") and some are long-term goals ("I will support my children as they engage in post-secondary education," or "I will increase my level of cardiovascular fitness and flexibility"). I also know that my short-term goals and long-term goals often connect to each other. The decisions I make every day lead me toward my long-term aspirations. When I don't meet my daily goals, my long-term goals can temporarily suffer. When I recover the following day and make different choices, I can find my way again. This is the connection between the present and the future—a connection we need students to understand.

We want students to experience this same connection and begin their own move toward daily decision making that serves long-term dreams. By inviting learners to set daily goals and intentions that connect to longer-term outcomes, you can begin to develop their sense of efficacy over their lifetimes, both as learners and as human beings. Research by James Stronge and Leslie Grant (2014) asserts that goal setting helps students focus on specific learning goals, while also encouraging them to seek academic challenges. Goal setting also makes clear the connection between learning in the immediate moment and long-term, future accomplishments. Research by Alexander Usher and Nancy Kober (2012) reminds us that goal setting must work to alter a student's perception of their own abilities in order to have a truly positive effect over time. Short- and long-term goal setting are powerful ways to make these connections explicit and tangible.

Grant Wiggins and Jay McTighe have long made the case for exploring goals and ideas that extend beyond the immediate. Their work with essential questions and understanding by design (UbD) (McTighe & Wiggins, 2013; Wiggins & McTighe, 2005) asserts that smaller skills and knowledge must connect to compelling questions and big ideas, worthy of long-term exploration. This is what gives daily learning meaning for students and what makes incremental steps part of the relevant and rich exploration of topics and ideas that matter in students' worlds.

Part of planning instruction is examining the importance of the goals we are developing with students. This is not always easy. When we ask ourselves *why*, of all the goals we could explore, this one matters, the answers are not always clear. Conversations with colleagues can help us get at the heart of our learning goals and really focus on the meaning we want students to gain from our daily lessons. Likewise, inviting students into discussions about what we are hoping to achieve together can help them connect short-term goals to long-term growth. It is helpful to make these connections explicit. Nordengren (2019) confirms this assertion, concluding, "Student-owned goal setting, undertaken through a variety of teaching styles and approaches, is a critical strategy for any school or district looking to create a culture of life-long learning." John Hattie and Gregory M. Donoghue (2016) also confirm the stages and benefits of this shared responsibility:

> The first step is to teach students to have goals relating to their upcoming work, preferably the appropriate mix of achieving and deep goals, ensure the goals are appropriately challenging and then encourage students to have specific intentions to achieve these goals. Teaching students that success can then be attributed to their effort and investment can help cement this power of goal setting, alongside deliberate teaching. (pp. 18–19)

Helping students make connections between their goals and achievement is critical. Sometimes an explanation can do the trick. For example, in English language arts, we might say:

> *"Today, we are going to work on your individual listening goals. Please find these goals in your data notebooks and review what you are currently working on. Turn to a partner and commit to the specific goal that will guide your efforts today. Please remember that your listening goals are part of your development as effective communicators in a variety of contexts. Whether you are an employer listening to your employee's concerns or a parent listening to your child's worries, these skills will define what you accomplish in these important moments."*

Linkages that may seem obvious to us may not be as obvious to students. To help students avoid over-compartmentalizing skills and knowledge, we need to intentionally engage in the kinds of conversations that explicitly connect short-term goal setting and a daily focus on specific tasks to long-term growth and achievement across learning contexts.

Characteristics of Strong Goals

Whether the goals we are inviting students to establish are daily and short-term or broader and long-term, the characteristics of strong goals can guide learners. These characteristics reflect the research guiding the attributes of SMART goals (Doran, 1981) in combination with my own classroom experiences. Characteristics of strong goals include the following.

- **Realistic, attainable, and challenging:** This means that students' daily goals may not always be the same. Rather, these goals can respond to students' most immediate needs.
- **Desirable and important:** This means that the goals matter to students.
- **Student driven:** This means that students have some autonomy in selecting their goals. However, goal selection is always grounded in evidence. For example, students will need to support goal choice based on evidence within their own data or artifacts (possibly in their data notebooks or portfolios). The analysis process (discussed in the previous chapter) should guide decision making.
- **Familiar:** This means students are familiar with both the success criteria and the actions they might take to achieve proficiency.
- **Choice in stakeholder support:** This means students have some choice in who will help them when they need it. It also means they understand that support is normal and desirable, even for highly successful people.
- **Varied:** This means that goals address both academic needs and social-emotional needs. This also means students are responsible for both their short-term and long-term growth.
- **Mastery based and tangible:** This means goals are based on the actual contexts in which students learn and determining success is based on specific targets and success criteria (not opinions and perceptions alone).

Now that we've identified the characteristics of strong learning goals, let's consider who owns these goals.

Ownership of Goals

There is no question that goals guide formal education. There are the learning goals prescribed for our students by governing bodies, goals articulated within curricular documents, and goals crafted by schools and systems. Rarely can a teacher open a resource without goals forming the structure of lessons and activities. Indeed, striving toward goals makes perfect sense when the work of people within education is to prepare learners for a future state.

Things become a little more challenging when we begin to ask ourselves who should actually *own* these goals. We could make a case for each person within a system to be responsible for certain goals. System or district leaders are accountable to system goals; school leaders are responsible for building goals.

Teachers are employed to achieve goals, certainly, but the inseparable relationship between teachers and learners supports the notion that goals should be co-owned. Learning goals specifically impact students—we expect students to meet specific skills and understanding as result of the work we do in the classroom. Therefore, it seems logical to engage and involve students in these educational goals. When everyone is working toward the same achievement measures, the chances of reaching these goals increases. It is for this reason that data notebooks and other self-assessment tools must focus on the skill of goal setting by students, based on their own strengths and needs.

So how autonomous should students be in setting their own goals? There is no question that allowing learners to set their own goals may cause apprehension. We worry that the goals they select might not be rigorous enough or based on the grade-level requirements for learning. We might also worry that students will set goals that are unattainable because they are unrealistic in their expectations for themselves. We might worry that if we don't control students' goals, we will not reach our expectations as educators. These concerns are valid and are worth acknowledging in order to move toward increased autonomy for learners.

Instead of thinking about student goal setting as *either* something learners control *or* something you control, imagine a less binary approach. First, in order to ensure equity for learners, we must commit to the grade-level goals that we identify as essential for each and every student. These goals are non-negotiable and form the foundation of student goal setting. For example, every learner in sixth grade will learn to support their ideas with strong, relevant evidence. Every student also will be able to solve complex mathematical word problems related to a variety of concepts. Both teachers and students are responsible for demonstrating these skills, and they represent long-term goal setting. We can help students understand that our work, as teachers, is to ensure everyone learns these important things—that this is *our job*.

However, in the short term, students can have tremendous autonomy in how they reach these goals. In this way, short-terms goals become *their job*. Students can select which strategies they will use as they learn to support their ideas and solve mathematics problems. They can choose which learning environments will work best for them (for example, working alone, working with others, working in silence, or working with music), what kinds of supports they might need (for example, anchor charts, peer mentors, and additional practice time), and how they might show their proficiency (for example, on a test, in a project, or through a video). Teachers and students can work together to discover the best ways to engage in new content, practice developing skills, and share learning.

When we work with data notebooks, portfolios, and other self-assessment tools, it is important to consider our learners' developmental nature. High school students can handle increased responsibility over their learning decisions and need accurate exposure to the consequences of those decisions so they can truly reflect on the choices they make day to day. Expecting high school students to set formal goals with descriptive actions is not unreasonable. Inviting these learners into conversations about learning preferences and approaches is a great time investment, since these students are fast approaching a time when they will be solely responsible for these kinds of decisions in post-secondary education, work environments, and daily contexts.

However, this level of formality and depth is unrealistic for our youngest students. Instead, teachers can view the act of setting goals as far more short term and emergent. Teacher-guided conversations can invite even the youngest students to begin to practice the crtitical skill of metacognition (awareness and understanding of one's own thought processes). In *The Metacognitive Student*, Richard K. Cohen, Deanne Kildare Opatosky, James Savage, Susan Olsen Stevens, and Edward P. Darrah (2021) offer the idea of SELf-questions as a way to kick-start this process, with a focus on academic and social problem solving as well as emotional problem solving. Practicing these metacognitive skills in a variety of contexts helps learners become increasingly comfortable with thinking about their thinking. For example, conversation starters like, "Did you notice what happened when you decided to _____? Tell me what you saw. If you could try again, what would you do the same? What would you do differently?" can help students think about their actions as decisions. This immediate action-reflection cycle helps students who are just learning to slow down long enough to consider options. For elementary and middle school students, teachers need to focus on the subskills of self-assessment (described in chapter 2, page 19) via developing self-assessment strength. Helping students notice and describe experiences, consider the feelings and actions of others, and see their choices as decisions is an important first step in learning to become proficient self-assessors.

The critical element in self-assessment for all ages is to present this kind of individual goal setting as a way to explore *who students are as learners*—which strategies work best, what conditions support their growth, and which processes lead them to long-term goals. Goal setting in this context is an investigation of learning, and it allows teachers and students to *work together* to create learning experiences that support their development. Even students who can independently identify what they need to work on sometimes need advice and guidance on how to go about improvement. This is how teachers and students can co-construct learning plans and learners can maintain some autonomy over their own learning journeys.

How to Make This Work

Predictable routines are the foundation of confident goal setting. When students experience some control over how they engage in learning and they also experience predictable processes for reflecting on the success of these approaches, they will realize the role they play in their educational journey. Teaching students the power of autonomy is part of building independent, capable learners.

However, it is essential we acknowledge that predictable form without substance can translate into goal setting that becomes another task for teachers to do. For example, giving students the same goal-setting template over and over without structuring in time for consistent analysis and reflection on tangible documentation (data or artifacts) can make goal setting feel disconnected from actual evidence and the resulting decision making that supports growth. That being said, it can be difficult to shift responsibility for decision making from the teacher alone to a community of learners. Students may find this transition challenging, especially if it is new to them and if they have achieved success (high grades or permission to be passive) when the teacher made all the decisions.

I have had students who actively resisted my request for decision making and subsequent responsibility for outcomes. I recall one learner in particular who stated, "Isn't that your job?" This reaction speaks to a system that has explicitly taught and then reinforced the idea that students are passive recipients of adult decision making. For some students, this is very comfortable because ultimately, they are never responsible for outcomes when they had no part in the original decision making. This is why making goal setting an authentic part of classroom learning is so critical. This isn't easy work, but it is important work.

In cases in which students seem to resist taking responsibility for decision making, there are a few approaches to consider in order to shift the narrative of student decision making from passive to active.

- **Let students set their own goals:** As I explain in *Softening the Edges: Assessment Practices That Honor K–12 Teachers and Learners* (2017), "No one loves being told what they need to fix and how they should do it every time they try something new. Taking risks is directly tied to retaining responsibility for the outcomes" (p. 135).

- **Work with students toward selecting goals that are truly meaningful for them:** This might require supplementary conversations with students about what interests them, what their dreams are for themselves, what excites them, what challenges they enjoy, and how they prefer learning to look and sound. These kinds of conversations illustrate the importance of relationships and a strong understanding between teachers and students. When you rush to goals without developing authentic relationships with students, they might assume that all decision making rests with you.

- **Ensure the stakes are low:** Limit student goal setting initially to specific subject areas and in relation to learning experiences that do not hold high stakes for students. Learning a new skill always goes better when students care about what they are doing and trust that their errors will not result in embarrassment or failure.

- **Build in meaning for students:** When students already possess a level of intrinsic interest in self-assessment and the context for self-assessment (the learning), their investment makes the process natural. Try to build in time to discuss how the learning might hold meaning for both teachers and students.

- **Ensure students experience quick wins as they practice goal setting:** Focus on goals that are very short-term and have a high chance of success. This makes the process seem productive from the outset.

- **Reinforce the message that goal setting is about taking specific actions and not a criticism of who learners are as people:** When this process and the agency required is new to students, they may interpret it is an attempt to improve them and not as a way to grow their learning. This difference must be clear to students.

- **Celebrate, celebrate, celebrate:** Too often, goal setting in any context seems to be more about fixing things than about making gains. Ensure the process feels good.

For students who have become disenfranchised with education, this shared responsibility for goal setting can feel even more challenging. Students may be actively resisting any kind of co-construction because it doesn't fit their story of who they are or who they want to be at school. In these cases, the resistance you may be experiencing moves beyond goal setting and your level of support, so intervention may need to be more intense. These students might be struggling with safety and security needs (physical, emotional, social, or intellectual), so we might focus on developing these areas before focusing on goal setting specifically.

Where to Start

Sometimes, when exploring a complex process like goal setting, it is helpful to focus on the very first steps we should take to begin. While the following four steps are not comprehensive, they are a way to begin this process if you are looking for a starting point.

1. Begin with a simple prompt before a product or performance is complete. Ask, "If your product or performance got even better tomorrow, what would you have done to make that happen?" Connect a future state to decision making.

2. Explicitly acknowledge strengths and remind students that part of goal setting is continuing actions we already know are successful. Move students away from the idea that goals are always about fixing mistakes.

3. Engage the class in group brainstorm sessions. Ask, "What strategies can we suggest for growing this skill? How might we enhance the quality of our products or performances?" Help students exercise their decision-making muscles.

4. Introduce a sample of a product or performance and invite students to offer suggestions for growth. Give them time to imagine a new outcome. Give time for students to share ideas and add to their toolboxes.

TOOLS TO SUPPORT SELF-ASSESSMENT

The following templates and tools can provide a framework for goal setting. Many of the elements are the same from sample to sample but the format shifts a little. Some are more appropriate for early elementary students, and some are better for upper elementary, middle school, or high school students. Teachers may use these templates alongside student artifacts and data, during or after a learning experience. As described in chapter 2 on documentation (page 19), having tangible artifacts, such as work samples, photographs, or video clips that can remind students of decisions they make and the resulting outcomes of those decisions, is helpful in making goal setting successful. In addition, making success criteria clear and available is important as well.

> **"Reflecting on Competencies" reproducible (page 84):** This tool invites students in grades 4–12 to connect short-term goals to broader competencies (for example, communication, collaboration) and provide evidence from their documentation for their decisions.

> **"Today's Goal" reproducible (page 85):** This tool asks students at any grade level to set quick, short-term goals for the day, and then reflect on evidence of success.

> **"Short- and Long-Term Goals" reproducible (page 86):** This tool asks students at any grade level to connect short-term goals to long-term goals.

> **"Reflecting and Goal Setting: English Language Arts" reproducible (page 87):** This tool is for students in grades 9–12 (although it could be simplified for earlier grades). It invites them to reflect on decisions they made during an English language arts unit. There is a heavy emphasis on the term *learning decisions*, which connects students to the idea of personal responsibility.

> **"Connecting Long-Term Goals to Short-Term Targets" reproducible (page 88):** This tool invites students to focus on a specific long-term academic goal and then track the individual, short-term targets that are part of developing the more longitudinal goal. At the end, students are asked to find evidence

(label or tag) for each target within their data notebook or portfolio. Students and teachers also can use this template to identify celebrations and needs.

> - **"My Goals" reproducible (page 89):** This tool can help students in any grade level and subject area set both short- and long-term goals. It helps them decide which kind of goals to focus on and what will indicate success. It also asks students to consider decisions they might need to make in order to reach those goals.
> - **"Goal Setting During Exploration" reproducible (page 90):** Students can use this tool to help them begin to set goals, articulate their success criteria, and plan for the next steps of their learning. Students can store this tool in a data notebook or portfolio and use it later for reflection and planning. You can also use this tool to design supports for students.
> - **"Daily Goal Setting" reproducible (page 91):** Students can use this tool each day or a few times each week to focus on daily decision making. They can share it with you to help guide supports and responsive instruction.
> - **"Reflecting and Goal Setting Prior to Sharing Learning With Others" reproducible (page 92):** This tool invites students to reflect on their efforts and determine the degree to which they are ready for sharing with others (a small or large audience). It brings students back to their goals and their success criteria to ensure readiness for sharing. Students can store completed versions in data notebooks or portfolios.
> - **"Daily Decision Making" reproducible (page 93):** You can use this tool to remind students of the options available to them in a longer-term learning context, and that there are several ways to get to growth and learning. It's also useful to group students who share similar actions.
> - **"Reaching My Goal" reproducible (page 94):** This tool includes language that may be more accessible to students in grades 2–8. Students in grades K–1 may need some guided support. This tool asks students to select a goal and reflect on parts of the goal that may feel easier than other parts. The focus on "tricky parts" allows you to work with students to anticipate and plan for challenges.
> - **"My Assessment Record" reproducible (page 95):** This tool is most applicable to students who may be examining specific scores in relation to artifacts. When students are looking at data sets, they can select specific data to inform goal setting. Students also can use this template with work samples, when scores are attached. The implication is that regardless of the score, there are always next steps to take.
> - **"It's All Down to Decisions: Monitoring Goals" reproducible (page 96):** This tool asks students at any grade level to frequently reflect on decision making and set goals that reflect which decisions were effective and which weren't.

QUESTIONS TO GUIDE CONVERSATION AND REFLECTION

On your own or as a part of a collaborative team, consider and discuss the following eight reflective questions.

1. Who makes decisions about long-term goals? Who decides what the day's goals will be?
2. How clear are students about the goals that guide learning each day? Do they have crystal clear understanding about the skills they are developing and why they are engaged in specific learning experiences?
3. How often do students reflect on the decisions they have made? How often do they experience the results of strategic decisions? To what degree do students see themselves as agents of change in the classroom?
4. Where are learning goals visible in the classroom and school? How tangible are these goals?

5. To what degree are daily learning goals connected to broader, more long-term goals or compelling questions? Do students understand how their daily learning fits into a larger plan?
6. How often is goal setting embedded into classroom instruction? When does it happen most often and least often? Why? To what degree do my students understand its importance?
7. How do students come to understand their strengths? Are these strengths connected to the goals they set and the decisions they make?
8. How do students respond to goal setting in their current context? What does this response tell me?

Reflecting on Competencies

Name: _____   Date: _____

Your learning this year is helping you develop important competencies that are important for life both inside and outside school. Follow the steps below.

1. Decide which competency you would like to focus on in your next unit of study.
2. Consider the smaller skills within the competency you will be working on developing. For example, you may select communication as your competency and then the specific skills of listening during group work and supporting your written responses fully.
3. Explain why you chose those specific skills.
4. Describe evidence that you are already growing in these areas.
5. Describe the things you may need to do to enhance these skills even more.

Competency focus (long-term goals):	
Communication	Social responsibility
Critical thinking	Positive and personal cultural identity
Creative thinking	Personal awareness and responsibility

Skill (or skills) within the competency that I am focusing on right now (short-term goals):

Reason for choosing this focus (short-term goal):

Evidence of my growth so far (decisions that are working well):

Things I still need to work on, and how I plan to do them:

Student Self-Assessment © 2022 Solution Tree Press • SolutionTree.com
Visit **go.SolutionTree.com/assessment** to download this page.

Today's Goal

Name: _____ Date: _____

Begin by setting a goal for class today. At the end of class, make time to reflect on your success.

My goal today:

Evidence of my success:

If I did not meet my goal, what do I need to do to make sure I meet it?

Student Self-Assessment © 2022 Solution Tree Press • SolutionTree.com
Visit **go.SolutionTree.com/assessment** to download this page.

Short- and Long-Term Goals

Name: _____ Date: _____

Select a long-term goal you have been working on in this course. Next, select short-term goals (things you will work on each day) to get you to the long-term goal.

My long-term goal:

Short-term goals that will get me there:

Student Self-Assessment © 2022 Solution Tree Press • SolutionTree.com
Visit **go.SolutionTree.com/assessment** to download this page.

Reflecting and Goal Setting: English Language Arts

Name: _____ Date: _____

Note: Do not fill out this self-assessment until you are finished with the entire unit.

Self-assessment and goal setting are important skills that you need to practice. Consider your learning decisions carefully and support your ideas fully. Use the checklist for potential learning decisions you might make if you are unsure.

Learning decisions I made in this unit that led to successful results and that I will continue to make are:

Learning decisions I will make differently next time to get closer to my goals are:
- ☐ Summarize what I read after each chapter
- ☐ Create notes or draw images about key elements of what I am reading
- ☐ Spend extra time during pre-writing brainstorming ideas
- ☐ Do more research before writing
- ☐ Talk through my ideas with a friend or mentor
- ☐ Read my work aloud to note places where phrasing is awkward
- ☐ Stop to reread, research, or imagine the action when I struggle with comprehension; slow down
- ☐ Set a timer and work for shorter periods of time with breaks in between each session
- ☐ Generate questions
- ☐ Spend extra time considering my main message
- ☐ Use a graphic organizer
- ☐ Use a voice-to-text app to listen to passages or write my own passages
- ☐ Use editing software to check my grammar and spelling
- ☐ Use images to help me write descriptively
- ☐ Use other texts as a guide for my own work
- ☐ Adjust the length and complexity of my sentences
- ☐ Work on using descriptive and interesting language (use a thesaurus to enhance vocabulary)
- ☐ Create a checklist by dividing a task into chunks
- ☐ Examine the criteria before, during, and after an assignment
- ☐ Try several different approaches before choosing the most effective one
- ☐ Read aloud
- ☐ Focus on selecting options that interest me when I can
- ☐ Ask for help from the teacher
- ☐ Other decisions: _____

Student Self-Assessment © 2022 Solution Tree Press • SolutionTree.com
Visit **go.SolutionTree.com/assessment** to download this page.

Connecting Long-Term Goals to Short-Term Targets

Name: _____ Date: _____

Write your long-term learning goal for this unit. Underneath, write smaller targets that you will practice and learn as part of moving toward the larger goal. Use the checklist of targets to monitor your strengths. As you show evidence of strength, check off the target. Label your evidence of target achievement in your data notebook or portfolio samples.

Long-Term Learning Goal:

Tracking Targets (Short-Term Goals):

I can:

- [ ] _____
- [ ] _____
- [ ] _____
- [ ] _____
- [ ] _____
- [ ] _____
- [ ] _____

I have shown my skill with this goal in relation to:

- [ ] _____
- [ ] _____
- [ ] _____
- [ ] _____
- [ ] _____
- [ ] _____
- [ ] _____

Label evidence within your portfolio with the short- and long-term goals the sample reflects.

Student Self-Assessment © 2022 Solution Tree Press • SolutionTree.com
Visit **go.SolutionTree.com/assessment** to download this page.

My Goals

Name: _____ Date: _____

My goals for the (circle one): Day / Week / Month / Year

To get better at _____, I could (brainstorm a list):

Some things I am definitely going to start doing are:

Some things I definitely need to stop doing are:

I commit to taking these actions by this date:

I will know I am getting better when:

Student Self-Assessment © 2022 Solution Tree Press • SolutionTree.com
Visit **go.SolutionTree.com/assessment** to download this page.

Goal Setting During Exploration

Name: _____ Date: _____

As you begin to focus on your product or performance, you will make some decisions to get started. Think about what you are trying to create, which materials or resources will help you get started, which prior skills or knowledge you already hold, and what your first steps will be. Your decisions may change as you go, but it is always a good idea to have a plan in the beginning.

Learning goals I plan to address:			
My Goal (I am going to try to . . . because . . .)	**Materials and Resources** (I think I might need . . . to get started.)	**Prior Knowledge and Skills** (I already know . . . ; I can already do . . .)	**Action Steps** (I am still wondering . . . ; to get started, I will need to . . .)

Criteria for Success

I will know I am experiencing success when:

I will know I need to rethink my plan if:

Student Self-Assessment © 2022 Solution Tree Press • SolutionTree.com
Visit **go.SolutionTree.com/assessment** to download this page.

Daily Goal Setting

Name: _____ Date: _____

At the beginning of class, please fill out the first two questions. Really consider what you are hoping to accomplish. At the end of class, return to this template and reflect on what happened and whether your actions moved you closer to your goals.

What I am trying to create, solve, design, practice, or invent today:

How I will know I am successful (criteria):

Date	What did I try today?	What were the results?	Did it get me closer to my goal?

My next steps are:

Student Self-Assessment © 2022 Solution Tree Press • SolutionTree.com
Visit **go.SolutionTree.com/assessment** to download this page.

Reflecting and Goal Setting Prior to Sharing Learning With Others

Name: _____ Date: _____

Use this tool to reflect on your efforts and determine how much you are ready to share with others.

My goal for this work:

My anticipated audience:

Criteria for Success	Current Strengths	What I Still Need to Do to Get Ready

From my audience, I need:

I think I will be ready to share on (date):

Student Self-Assessment © 2022 Solution Tree Press • SolutionTree.com
Visit **go.SolutionTree.com/assessment** to download this page.

Daily Decision Making

Name: _____ Date: _____

Think about your next steps for meeting your goals. Write what you need to do to meet those goals.

After today, my next steps will include:

- ☐ Self-assess and set a new goal
- ☐ Revise my work
- ☐ Restart
- ☐ Ask for help with _____
- ☐ Collaborate with _____ (name)
- ☐ Do a little more research
- ☐ See my teacher for a mini-lesson on _____
- ☐ Start something new
- ☐ Submit for feedback
- ☐ Submit for summative assessment
- ☐ Gather these additional materials: _____, _____

Any additional items, materials, or people I need to help me accomplish these next steps:

Reaching My Goal

Name: _____ Date: _____

Fill out the following questions to set a goal. Think about each question carefully.

My goal:

Target date: _____

How I will know I am successful:

This goal matters to me because:

The strengths I have that will help me reach this goal are:

Things that could get a little tricky:

What I am going to do when things get tricky:

Student Self-Assessment © 2022 Solution Tree Press • SolutionTree.com
Visit **go.SolutionTree.com/assessment** to download this page.

My Assessment Record

Use this table to track your scores on each assessment. Begin by identifying what the focus for the assessment was and what score(s) you received. Next, reflect on areas of strength and areas of need and what your goal(s) will be, moving forward.

Name:			Subject:
Date	**Assessment Focus**	**Score**	**Reflection (Strengths and Needs) and Goal**
Example: Nov. 12	Simplifying fractions	8/10	Strengths: Knowing how to simplify Needs: Simplifying enough Goal: Increase my skill of knowing when a fraction is truly simplified. I will spend extra time checking to make sure the fractions cannot be simplified any further.

Student Self-Assessment © 2022 Solution Tree Press • SolutionTree.com
Visit **go.SolutionTree.com/assessment** to download this page.

It's All Down to Decisions: Monitoring Goals

Name: _____ Date: _____

Existing Goal:

Using your sample or samples as a guide, reflect on your efforts in achieving quality. What strategies did you try to reach your goal? Did these strategies work? Will you continue this goal or move to something new, based on your evidence?

I have tried the following:

The following worked:

The following did not work:

My next goal:

CHAPTER 5

Celebrating Growth

*It is imperative that teachers help learners build a repertoire of success—
a history filled with evidence of capabilities—so that when learners do have difficult tasks,
their hopefulness can fuel their stamina, and they can persevere in the face of a challenge.*
—Cassandra Erkens, Tom Schimmer, and Nicole Dimich

The teacher asks his students to take out their data notebooks and turn to the Reflections section near the back. He reminds them to start by placing the date at the top of the page and then waits for them to get organized.

"Today, you are going to take a little time to celebrate your growth," he announces. "I have watched you learn so much in this unit, and I want to make sure you see it, too. To guide your reflection today, I have two prompts I would like you to consider." He turns and points to the chart paper on the stand at the front of the room. He reads the prompts aloud: "Prompt number one: Looking back at the success criteria for this unit and the evidence in your data notebook, describe two specific skills you have improved in this unit. Support your reflection with evidence from your data or your artifacts."

The teacher turns back to the class and clarifies, "So, if you notice that you improved in the skill of explaining your thinking, using details and examples, then mention this criterion. Follow up with a phrase like, 'I know this because . . . ,' and then find evidence in your assessments and data that supports this statement. Maybe you have feedback from me or a classmate that states this. Perhaps your responses on our last assignment demonstrate this. Maybe you have evidence in your drafts that shows you were thinking about this when you were planning your last essay. Evidence can come from several places." He pauses and lets this example sink in. "What questions do I need to answer right now?"

A student raises her hand. "What if I just know I have gotten better, but I don't have evidence?"

"Great question," the teacher responds. "There are times when we just feel success, and it might be challenging to find evidence to support our feelings. This is called intuition, and it is a good place to start. However, our intuitions come from our experiences and our knowledge. While we may not be able to locate evidence immediately, somewhere in your efforts in this unit, you have shown this growth. I am challenging you to find evidence because it is there. You might have to be like a detective. It is possible that your evidence might also come from your memories. If you can remember an example that occurred while we were practicing and exploring in class, that counts. Describe that moment."

Another student raises his hand, "What if I don't have any strengths? I can't think of anything that has improved."

"I'm glad you asked me that question. In fact, your question is one of the reasons we are making time to celebrate. I can guarantee that each of you has grown in the required skills of this unit. That was our job together. We worked on developing knowledge and skills, and our last assessment showed that." He pauses and makes sure the student is absorbing his assurances. He continues, "Do you remember at the beginning of the unit, when we listed actions that were important when we were doing every assignment, no matter what the topic was? We also were going to practice things like. . . ."

The teacher turns to the board and begins to list the skills as he says them aloud, "Trying an answer, even when we are unsure; writing our thinking in complete sentences; asking good questions before and during learning; seeking support from others; making time to brainstorm before responding; reading texts carefully and summarizing ideas." He turns back to face the class. "These are also skills worth celebrating, even though they aren't the specific skills and success criteria we were working on in this subject."

The teacher returns to the chart paper and reads the second prompt aloud: "Prompt number two: How would you like to celebrate today?" He turns and reminds students what he means. "Remember that we have a list of celebration options to choose from. Maybe you want to send an email to a family member. Perhaps you would like to confer with me or Principal Baggart. You might want to make yourself a celebration card. Any of the options are available. Focus on one that will actually mean something to you."

The teacher anticipates offering a little time for this reflection. Learning to acknowledge growth is a skill needing development, just like any other. He looks forward to reading his students' thoughts.

RESPOND TO THE SCENARIO

Answer the following questions using information from the preceding scenario.
- Who is making decisions in this scenario? What are they deciding?
- Why is celebration an important stage of self-assessment? Why might this be important for these students and this teacher?
- What is the role of the teacher in this scenario?

Everyone needs to feel like they are doing things right—making good decisions and accomplishing goals. In schools, this need exists for both teachers and students. However, it can sometimes be difficult to focus on the positives because the education system often focuses on the negatives, or learning gaps, instead. This is natural when the purpose of education and assessment within it is to analyze student learning and determine the degree to which there is a gap between the current state and the goals students are trying to achieve. I often remind teachers that their work rests in this deficit, in the space before proficiency. This is why it is such a strong inclination, when faced with student artifacts, to head right in and identify mistakes. We correct errors and calculate scores. It feels like our job!

However, there is a downside to this approach. When we make it our business to look for gaps, they can become all we see. We may approach an assessment with optimism, only to feel quickly defeated because we recognize that students are not yet where we want them to be. We may feel frustration with students because they have not yet learned what we believed we taught effectively. Students very quickly pick up on this pattern of deficit thinking and reflect that in their language following an assessment experience. After returning an assessment, we may hear questions like, "How many did you get wrong?" or "What did she say you still needed to do?" There can be too great a fixation on the work before us, and we forget to acknowledge the distance we have travelled.

Celebrating growth is essential for students' mental well-being. Imagine starting every day with a list of what students were doing *right*. Instead of listing the mistakes we notice students make on an assessment, we can offer learners a list of strengths (generated from the work of every single student) and ask them to examine their assessment and select which strengths belong to them. Perhaps we make time for students to examine their data notebooks or portfolios and list the skills they *do not* need to work on because they have already mastered them. These approaches instill optimism, confidence, and student investment within a classroom culture; they communicate that there are things worth celebrating. It is through growth that students develop resilience. They come to understand that their current state is temporary, and challenges can and will turn into strengths with the right kinds of decisions.

This approach is healthy for teachers, too. Think of a student strength as one less thing you have to do. If students possess the strength of attempting a question even though they may not be sure of their response, this is one less challenge educators have to address.

Teachers can pick up right at the response and not need to work on helping a student take a risk when confronted with uncertainty. If a learner demonstrates two of three targets within a complex goal, teachers must create time to celebrate the acquisition of those two skills—two less things for both teachers and students to do. On top of that, instruction led to success. This is definitely worth celebrating.

Celebrations allow us to invite our past journey into decisions about our next steps. We can encourage students to set two-part goals: first, they list the skills they already possess and wish to continue; second, they select a skill or two that need attention. As Dimich (2015) reminds us, "Students who are invested recognize when they feel confident as well as when they feel unsure" (p. 11). We nurture this self-awareness through the act of analyzing, reflecting, and celebrating. We have to acknowledge our past before we can move into the future.

Sometimes past decisions do not serve our goals, but often they do. We want students to recognize when they make good choices. Only then do we invite them to consider which decisions led to less desirable results. Both states are important to their future decisions, which must reflect an understanding of their successes and challenges. Strength and need are two sides of the same coin, and both are necessary to sustain learning, even when the going gets tough. Tomlinson (2005) reminds us that "students' attitudes about learning and about themselves as learners are of great importance in establishing, maintaining, and developing students' commitment to the learning process" (p. 263). Celebration is part of building commitment.

In this chapter, you will explore several considerations for self-assessment as related to celebrating student growth and learning, including how to ensure celebrations are meaningful by connecting them to tangible goals and student values. You also will learn strategies for how to make celebrations effective in the context of classroom learning by embracing student input and feedback, celebrating classwide and individual achievements, and honoring short-term goals as well as growth toward long-term goals. At the end of the chapter, you will find practical templates and tools to help you and your students engage in meaningful celebrations, along with steps for where to start and questions for conversation and reflection with colleagues and students.

Considerations for Self-Assessment

How we celebrate learner growth in our classrooms needs to be as individualized as the data on which we base celebrations. What each student considers a success and how the teacher acknowledges each learner will differ from individual to individual. For this reason, celebrations need to be tied tightly to a strong understanding of who students are and what they value. Consider the following grounds for celebration and how to take a nuanced approach to these celebrations.

Grounds for Celebration

How do we know when it makes sense to celebrate? While the answer may seem obvious, it is not. We as teachers can't celebrate everything, or that's all we would do. Learning happens every single day—or at least that is the goal. So we have to have as intentional an approach to celebration as we do to analysis and goal setting. We also may want to celebrate things that don't actually matter to students, which could make celebrations feel tokenistic or teacher centered. So, we have to celebrate when it makes sense to both teachers and students. In this way, celebration is as co-constructed as the initial documentation and data collection. Let's consider how we will know when we have grounds for celebration.

First, it is helpful to explicitly connect celebrations to tangible goals. The previous chapters have articulated the importance of selecting the most important academic and behavioral goals on which to focus and monitor. We have explored ways to invite students to collect documentation and analyze it for patterns, trends, strengths, and needs. Chapter 4 (page 71) focused on how to shift goal-setting responsibilities to students so they can practice making decisions and reflecting on the results of those decisions in relation to their goals. If we have successfully done all this, celebrating growth will flow naturally from this process. The through line from goal, to actions and decisions, to reflection, to celebration or next steps will be clear and tangible.

Helping students navigate this process and develop independence as self-assessors is an important educational priority. Perhaps a seventh-grade student has been working on playing strategically during a specific game in physical education or mathematics.

This learner may have examined video footage to look for evidence of strong decision making and may have set a goal to play more defensively in the next series of games. When subsequent video footage demonstrates growth on this goal, it makes sense to explicitly acknowledge this growth and how it connects to choices made by the learner. In this way, we are celebrating academic goals alongside the goal of becoming a strong self-assessor.

In a different example, a high school student may have written a mid-unit formative assessment in a social science class and analyzed it to identify their strengths and needs. The student may then, in cooperation with their teacher, set a goal to show greater proficiency on the review quiz in a week's time. With the support of the teacher, the student determines action steps and generates practice and study plans. When the review assessment occurs the following week and the student shows growth, celebration might follow, despite the fact that the student had not yet written their summative assessment. Goals can reflect growth in any number of ways, but alignment between goals and celebrations should be clear. Both teachers and students should understand the criteria for what constitutes success. In this example, the goal is not to do well on the summative assessment but rather to show greater proficiency on a future formative assessment. Presumably, summative proficiency follows, but the goal dictates when to acknowledge success (after the formative review quiz).

In an early elementary context, the process of formal goal setting may feel less pronounced and so might the corresponding celebration. Perhaps, during cooperative play, the teacher notices that a first-grade student is having difficulty sharing materials with others. The teacher may speak with the student about the need to share, and together, they may devise a way for the student to relinquish some of their materials to others. In the next iteration of cooperative play, when the teacher notices the young learner pause and hand over a toy or material to a peer, it makes sense for the teacher to make time to confer with the learner again to talk about and celebrate the different decision, showing student growth. Tying the celebration to the goal is important in guiding how celebration might occur in this case. It is important that the student connects the result of the new decision to a value they might hold (for example, a desire to make a friend happy or to feel good about sharing) rather than connecting the celebration to the teacher (for example, celebrating because it makes the teacher happy). We want the learner to understand the goal's purpose, not feel that the only time to celebrate is when it pleases the teacher. This would establish an unhealthy cycle of compliance and reward.

We want to celebrate the achievement of a short-term goal, a step taken in a journey toward a long-term goal, or a decision made in service of something that holds value for learners. In some classrooms, the goals belong to the teacher and may be unclear to learners. The teacher makes all subsequent decisions in the classroom, and so, when celebrations occur, students might feel that the teacher is celebrating themself. True partnership is based on shared responsibility. This is why it is important that students are partners in the decisions teachers make in the classroom. Authentic celebration feels best when everyone involved has a choice in the goals, is part of the journey, and can make decisions that lead to a positive outcome.

Students can use the "I Can Self-Assess!" reproducible (page 104) to identify the indicators of strong self-assessment or to track growth in each area.

It has to be said that not all students enjoy public celebration. While some learners cannot get enough of peers or adults learning of their success, other learners would like to keep their growth private. Therefore, a nuanced approach to celebration is necessary.

A Nuanced Approach to Celebration

In an attempt to acknowledge successful skill acquisition, you may make a celebration decision that actually discourages future efforts. This is why your approach to celebration has to be nuanced. You have to know your learners.

One of the most important things we can do with students is learn about their values. Understanding their values provides insight into which goals hold meaning for them and how they might like to celebrate once they achieve those goals. This is important because each student determines the worth of a goal and the worth of its celebration once they achieve it. The learner ultimately determines meaning. Authors Lauren Porosoff and Jonathan Weinstein (2018) explain it this way: "Meaning is not inherent in a thing, whether it's a pen, a work environment, or a school assignment. Meaning comes from our history relating to the thing" (p. 6). This means that we have to work at building a shared history with students, with the goals we set in the classroom, and with the ways we decide to celebrate those goals. We have to explore what matters most to students and why. We can't get to this kind of exploration without a concerted effort.

It is important to understand the difference between values and goals and how they connect, so we can make celebration decisions that honor the learners in your classroom. *Values* are "qualities of action that make life meaningful" (Porosoff & Weinstein, 2018, p. 6), while *goals* are a desired result or future outcome. In other words, goals drive our actions, while values give meaning to those actions and the goals they serve. Meaning is then connected to student investment. When we achieve the sweet spot of selecting goals that reflect student values and designing celebrations that hold authentic meaning, we have tapped into learning that matters.

In order to determine what matters to students, we should invite conversations that explore personal connections and then listen to learners. We might ask them questions about their preferences for celebration, public acknowledgment, and reflection. We might explore the kinds of activities that bring them joy and would be appropriate to incorporate into celebration. For example, does dancing feel joyful, and does it make sense to move in celebration of a goal? Does quiet time bring students joy, and could a celebration include quiet time at the end of a class period? Does it make sense to have a celebration checklist in the back of data notebooks where students add to the list of goals they achieve?

We also might want to design varied celebration experiences in the first few weeks of school and observe how students respond to those experiences. Some students may thrive on competition, and celebration would be strongly connected to winning a prize. Others may prefer to quietly reflect and experience internal pride. Yet others may enjoy receiving a card of acknowledgment from another person (for example, peer, teacher, mentor, friend, family member, community member). Some students may enjoy talking with peers about their achievements, while others may prefer written conversations. For some learners, a successful act of service is the ultimate celebration—

seeing the positive effects of their efforts on others. Learning our students' preferences and what seems to matter most to them can help us guide students to self-assessment practices and subsequent celebrations that reflect their values. Ultimately, students hold the key to nuanced celebrations. They can help us figure out how to acknowledge strength and growth in ways that encourage future efforts.

How to Make This Work

One way to collect the necessary information to design strong celebrations is to simply ask students for input and feedback. Teachers can give the reproducible templates listed in the next section to students to reflect on their personal preferences. In this way, teachers and students can more closely align celebrations with who they are celebrating. Teachers also can use the suggestions within the templates to experiment with and then reflect on the effects of the chosen celebration.

It is important to note that celebration can occur in varied circumstances, beyond individual students and individual goals. Sometimes celebrations might reflect classwide achievements (for example, we all were able to make text-to-self connections while reading), while other times the celebrations may focus on small groups of students (for example, this group of students wrote a dramatic presentation that fulfilled the success criteria). Additionally, data notebooks and portfolios facilitate not only the celebration of short-term goals but also an acknowledgment of growth toward long-term goals. This is why collecting multiple data sets and artifact samples allows celebration to occur at various times.

Where to Start

Sometimes, when exploring a complex process like celebration, it helps to focus on the very first steps we might take to begin. While the following six steps are not comprehensive, they are a way to begin this process if you are looking for a starting point.

1. Engage students in a class discussion about celebration, including why it is important, when it makes sense, and how it might occur.

Show the importance of celebration by spending time exploring it. Laugh, cheer, and focus on optimism. This may be one of the only times some students experience this.

2. Explore the difference between celebrating oneself and bragging. Invite students to share personal and cultural values in this regard and co-construct a shared understanding.

3. Examine student artifacts for strengths first. Resist looking for mistakes right away; focus on strengths.

4. Set personal goals to make time to offer students a quick acknowledgment, using something easy like a sticky note or a quick digital message (when appropriate). You might even mail letters of celebration home to great effect (one of my students framed his note).

5. Model self-reflection and celebration. Show students how to recognize moments worthy of celebration, and make time to explicitly acknowledge your own growth.

6. Audit your school's decisions around celebration. Explore who the school or class celebrates in ceremonies and events. Ask yourself how these decisions are made and how they affect the student body. Look through the lenses of equity, bias, confidence, growth mindset, and mission, vision, values, and goals. Ask students questions about their experiences with celebration and gather perceptions.

TOOLS TO SUPPORT SELF-ASSESSMENT

The following templates and tools can provide a framework for celebrating student growth and achievement in your classroom. Some are more appropriate for students in grades K–3, while others are more appropriate for upper elementary, middle school, or high school students.

> **"I Can Self-Assess!" reproducible (page 104):** This tool invites students of any age (with guidance in early elementary classrooms) to monitor their development of self-assessment skills. It also offers a comprehensive list of specific actions students should take as they develop this skill from year to year. Teachers and students can use this reflection tool to plan areas of focus for developing self-assessment skills. Of course, this tool also offers plenty of opportunities for celebration.

> **"Celebrations With Others" reproducible (page 105):** You can use this tool with students of any grade level. It invites learners to consider with whom they might like to celebrate their growth and success. Teachers and students can use this list through the year to guide celebrations.

> **"How I Would Like to Celebrate" reproducible (page 106):** You can use this tool with students at any grade level (with guidance in early elementary classrooms). It invites students to think about how they might like to be celebrated, so you can honor individual preferences.

> **"Celebration Time!" reproducible (page 107):** You can use this tool with students in any grade level. It invites students to identify what they are celebrating and why. They can write or draw their good news and then share it with the class.

QUESTIONS TO GUIDE CONVERSATION AND REFLECTION

On your own or as a part of a collaborative team, consider the following eight reflective questions.

1. How often is formal celebration a part of the classroom and school experience of students and teachers?
2. How does the staff celebrate growth? To what degree do the adults model celebration every day? What are staff celebrating?

3. What does my school or class celebrate? Who does my school or class celebrate? What does this communicate about our mission, vision, values, and goals? What does it communicate about equity and potential? What does it say about what matters most? Are these the messages I am trying to send?

4. How are personal celebrations different from public celebrations? Why might personal celebrations be important?

5. Who decides school and classroom celebrations? How might students make more decisions in this regard? Why might this be important?

6. How are relationships with students and celebrations connected? How might I or my school team enhance both?

7. Why are learning goals and success criteria so important to celebration? How do learning strategies and work habits connect to celebration? Are students clear about these aspects of learning? How are they made clear?

8. To what degree are students hopeful, confident, and resilient? How might celebrations support and encourage these qualities?

I Can Self-Assess!

Name: _____ Date: _____

Use the following checklist to monitor your self-assessment skills. Be sure you have evidence (in your data notebook or portfolio) to support your claims.

I am a strong self-assessor when I:

- ☐ Document my learning from beginning to end (through products, photos, video)
- ☐ Organize my documentation and data in a notebook, portfolio, or digital file
- ☐ Notice features and describe my data and artifacts
- ☐ Compare my efforts to success criteria
- ☐ Analyze my artifacts and data to identify my strengths
- ☐ Analyze my artifacts and data to identify my needs or areas for growth
- ☐ Remember and reflect on decisions I made while learning (use documentation to help)
- ☐ Decide whether my decisions led me toward or away from my goals
- ☐ Consider what matters to me (my values, my beliefs, my goals, my preferences)
- ☐ Set goals that matter to me
- ☐ Select actions that I think will get me closer to my goals
- ☐ Think about when and how I will try approaches and strategies
- ☐ Ask for support when I need it
- ☐ Accept failure and think about what decisions I could make that would get me to a different result
- ☐ Seek feedback from others
- ☐ Act on feedback that seems helpful in getting me to my goals
- ☐ Celebrate my successes
- ☐ Reflect on how I like to celebrate
- ☐ Respect, empathize, and show compassion for myself and others because I know life has both failure and success
- ☐ Revisit, review, and revise my products and performances

Add any additional self-assessment skills you can think of.

Student Self-Assessment © 2022 Solution Tree Press • SolutionTree.com
Visit **go.SolutionTree.com/assessment** to download this page.

Celebrations With Others

Name: _____ Date: _____

Sometimes, it is nice to share our successes with other people. Everyone has people who really matter to them and who would be happy to hear our good news. Take a moment and reflect on whom you might like to include in your celebrations.

- ☐ My family members' names:

- ☐ My friends' names:

- ☐ School personnel names:

- ☐ Community members' names:

- ☐ Pets' names:

- ☐ Mentors' or elders' names:

- ☐ Names of other important people in my life:

- ☐ List any other people you would like to celebrate with:

Student Self-Assessment © 2022 Solution Tree Press • SolutionTree.com
Visit **go.SolutionTree.com/assessment** to download this page.

How I Would Like to Celebrate

Name: _____   Date: _____

Everyone has their own way of celebrating successes, and how we celebrate connects to who we are as people. Take a moment and consider how you might like to celebrate when the time comes. Check off any ideas that appeal to you.

- ☐ Spoken words of acknowledgment (for example, specific description of what I did well or related to specific goals)
- ☐ Written acknowledgment (for example, a small note, a text, an email, or a letter)
- ☐ Tracking of targets (for example, checklists of things I am working on that I can use to monitor growth)
- ☐ Goal-setting sheets that include strengths, successes, and prior knowledge and skills
- ☐ Celebrations with family through notes, emails, phone calls, letters, or videos from me or my teacher
- ☐ Peer celebrations with classmates and friends
- ☐ Mentor celebration shared via email or phone call
- ☐ Selection and display of samples of growth with specific goal labels
- ☐ Established signals of celebration (for example, high five, cheer, thumbs up)
- ☐ Quiet conversations and conferences
- ☐ Celebration wall (a place to acknowledge successes)
- ☐ Goal jars to enter record of goal success—reflect and celebrate once a month
- ☐ Celebration page in data notebooks in which you list successes
- ☐ Strength-based role supports offered to peers ("Ask me for help with . . .")
- ☐ Class rewards (for example, dance-off or visiting time)
- ☐ Journaling celebrations (a chance to personally reflect on what is going well)
- ☐ A letter or card to myself
- ☐ Others:

Celebration Time!

Name: _____   Date: _____

It's time to celebrate! Use this sheet to describe your celebration.

Today, I am celebrating:

Why this is worth celebrating:

How I am celebrating:

Student Self-Assessment © 2022 Solution Tree Press • SolutionTree.com
Visit **go.SolutionTree.com/assessment** to download this page.

CHAPTER 6

Examining Age, Security, Families, and Other Factors

Without water drops, there can be no oceans; without steps, there can be no stairs; without little things, there can be no big things.

—Mehmet Murat Ildan

We have covered a lot of ground in this book about data notebooks and other self-assessment tools. We have explored the purpose of self-assessment and how we might help students document their story of learning, from beginning to end. We have learned how to facilitate the analysis of both data and artifacts and determine goals based on the information available. Lastly, we have investigated the importance of formal celebration and ways it might occur in our classrooms and schools. There are just a few additional things to consider before engaging students in self-assessment.

In this final chapter, we investigate how a learner's age impacts self-assessment in the classroom. We also examine why thinking about safety and privacy is an important step before beginning data notebooks and other self-assessment tools. We explore ways to engage families in these processes and why this is an important aspect of any assessment system. We clarify the role of the student in self-assessment and how this relates to but is different from the role of the teacher. Lastly, we discuss how to overcome common barriers that seem to prevent data notebooks, portfolios, and other self-assessment tools from being useful and effective.

Self-Assessment and Students in Early Elementary Classrooms

A very good friend of mine, who happens to be an expert early elementary teacher, asked me an important question that served as the catalyst for this section of the book: "How do we accomplish this with early elementary students?" It was a fair question, and the answer is important if this whole self-assessment thing is going to work. This is especially true because students in early elementary classrooms eventually become adults who need to be self-sufficient and adept at assessing their progress in relation to goals, so we have to begin to build these skills right from the outset. Most processes in this book support growth in both academic and behavioral outcomes and well as in the skill of self-assessment, but many of the templates and processes would be difficult for young learners to manage. So, we circle back to the question of how to successfully accomplish this with them.

To answer this question, you have to think about the capacity of grades K–3 students to engage in the complex skill of self-assessment. In other words, what is developmentally appropriate for this group of learners? And, which aspects of data notebooks and self-assessment can we teach students to a degree of independence? That is, we definitely do not want hordes of teachers spending hours each day making data notebooks for every learner in their classroom (and I know there are teachers out there who do this, with the best of intentions). Self-assessment has to emphasize the *self*, and so we need to select ways to develop key skills without taking over for students.

To respond to this query, we might consider the following.

1. Which aspects of daily learning might include opportunities for self-assessment?

109

2. Which aspects of self-assessment should we emphasize and develop? How can we break this process into smaller, manageable pieces?

3. When does it make sense to engage in self-assessment with younger students and under which conditions?

The following sections explore three topics that can help self-assessment live and grow in early elementary classrooms: (1) how teachers can narrow the focus of self-assessment to make it more easily accessible for young students, (2) how making time to develop the foundational skills of self-assessment can support overall student growth and confidence, and (3) how making time to honor emergent self-assessment opportunities allows you to embed the process within your classroom.

Narrowing the Focus

My friend and colleague, Nicole Dimich (2015), reminds teachers in her book *Design in Five: Essential Phases to Create Engaging Assessment Practice*, to select goals that focus on "essential-to-know, hard-to-teach, and hard-to-learn concepts" (p. 37).

In other words, when teachers feel stretched to address everything, they might consider investing the most time in those goals that are complex, rich, and worth working hard to ensure every students reaches. I love this list of qualities because they communicate the idea that educators can't do everything. Teachers must engage learners in numerous complex academic goals on top of the myriad other things they need to accomplish in any given day. When teachers believe they need to add on self-assessment processes for every classroom experience, it is understandable that they throw their hands up and say, "Enough!" However, when educators heed Dimich's advice, things make more sense.

Because early learning teachers are working on building the foundation of self-assessment skills, it makes the most sense to focus on a few important goals (hard to teach; hard to learn; worth interevention) and return to them more than once so students can practice making decisions and reflecting on the outcomes. So when we think about how to focus the time we spend on self-assessment, we want to ask ourselves which goals (academic, behavioral, or both) are complex, important in several contexts, and challenging for young learners to grasp. Perhaps we want to invite students to practice self-assessment skills in relation to navigating transitions. Or maybe we want to engage learners in self-assessment as they begin to read or speak with expression or listen to their peers during collaborative time. These kinds of goals are hard to teach, hard to learn, and teachers will definitely spend time practicing and reteaching when needed because these goals really matter in both the short and long terms.

Developing Foundational Skills

If you think back to chapter 2 (page 19), when the subskills of self-assessment were discussed, you can begin to think about self-assessment as a complex skill, and that the work of young students is to develop and refine some of those smaller subskills to build readiness for complex self-assessment processes. This means you might focus in kindergarten on developing the skills of noticing, remembering, and describing, for example. Perhaps data notebooks include simple data sets, and students focus on noticing key features of the data, describing what they see. When engaging in learning experiences, emphasize helping students remember things that have occurred in the near and distant past. For example, a colleague of mine arranged for me to visit her classroom dressed in silly clothing. I simply entered the room, walked around a little, and left. She then asked students to remember and describe me, practicing these important subskills.

As students move into first, second, and third grades, they continue to practice and refine these skills in increasingly complex situations. First- and second-grade students might notice features of two or more data sets, or third-grade students might consider ways to enhance how to represent data. Teachers should continue to help students refine these subskills by adding complexity to the contexts in which students are applying them.

Self-assessment is a difficult skill to master, and it requires more of students than simply setting a goal or looking at graphs. However, the subskills of self-assessment are important building block to developing strong and effective self-assessment processes, and early learning educators are laying the foundation for future years when they engage in this developmental work.

Capitalizing on Emergent Opportunities

The idea of forcing students in early elementary classrooms to sit and examine rubrics, fill out multi-step goal-setting sheets, and color graph after graph can make any early elementary teacher reconsider focusing on developing the skill of self-assessment. The formal nature of assessment processes in traditional classrooms has led us to believe that assessment can be time-consuming and painful. However, assessment that we use to advance learning and facilitate good decisions by teachers and students can be very organic in nature. In any classroom, but particularly in early elementary contexts, self-assessment might emerge from daily learning experiences and appear much less formal than one might think. Instead of sitting down with a text-heavy template, students might engage in reflection and planning in the moment and orally.

For example, imagine a first-grade student named Maya is working on the skill of making patterns and is using natural materials, such as pinecones and small rocks, to create various examples. The teacher, Ms. Juarez, notices that Maya sticks to patterns of two of each material repeated. Maya seems comfortable with counting by twos but is not experimenting with different kinds of patterns. Instead of asking Maya to stop and set a formal goal, Ms. Juarez engages Maya in a conversation, asking how she decides what her pattern will be. Ms. Juarez then introduces a third and fourth material and observes the pattern Maya makes. When Maya repeats the core pattern of two, Ms. Juarez invites her to think about other ways to make patterns, and even models an example with entirely different materials. Together, Ms. Juarez and Maya establish a goal of creating as many different patterns as possible with four materials. Ms. Juarez invites Maya to take a picture of each pattern with an iPad or draw each pattern she finds (documentation). Later, Ms. Juarez revisits Maya and asks her to reflect on (analyze) her success. Ms. Juarez invites her to count how many different patterns she discovers, referring her back to her documentation. Ms. Juarez then asks Maya to reflect on whether she thinks she found all the possibile patterns and with whom she might check to be sure. Ms. Juarez then invites Maya to set a new goal by adding more or different materials or introducing symbols like letter or numbers with which to create patterns.

This example illustrates the emergent and organic nature of self-assessment and goal setting with young students. Intentional and considered conversations are the core of early elementary instruction, and they work well for encouraging the youngest learners to slow down a little and think about their decisions and actions. This is not only developmentally appropriate, but it also reminds teachers that assessment does not have to live in print—it can emerge from observation and conversation, and as long as it informs good decision making, it is doing its job.

In building the ability of learners to reflect on their own decisions, teachers should focus on clarifying for young learners which aspects of future decisions will be their responsibility (for example, next time you work with a partner, you will share your materials) and which aspects will be the responsibility of the teacher (for example, I will make sure there are enough supplies for everyone to have what they need). The more we can specifically shift responsibility for future actions to our students, the greater the opportunity we have to develop efficacy and self-regulation.

Safety and Privacy

It is challenging to think about privacy when considering the very public endeavor of education. Sometimes it feels like everything teachers and students do in schools is a matter of public consideration and discourse. While this makes sense in some regard (in many North American schools, public taxes largely fund the K–12 education, and therefore, some could argue that this process is a matter of public interest), it's worth asking ourselves whether *everything* belongs in the public realm. Consider the importance of emotional and social safety for learners in making them comfortable enough to take risks and make mistakes. Consider the vulnerable position of students who have low confidence and limited success in traditional school environments. Consider the very human need to protect ourselves and have some aspects of our internal lives stay internal. Consider the important legal need to protect students within online, digital realms. Then consider the topics of data notebooks, portfolios, and self-assessment and the degree to which these processes may make students feel emotionally or socially unsafe as well as exposed and judged. It is this tension between public and private that makes this topic worth investigating.

Belinha de Abreu (2017) describes this tension when she states:

> In U.S. consumer culture, it is increasingly obvious that there is uncertainty and lack of knowledge on the idea of "privacy." Students acknowledge the term, but don't necessarily know where to draw the line. And the adults in students' lives share the same struggle.

When students document and then analyze their efforts as they learn, there will be times when their documentation reflects less than proficiency. We have already explored the importance of these interim steps in helping students take ownership of their decisions and the subsequent successes or failures. However, taking ownership of decisions is different from making them public. Considering and then explicitly sharing who will bear witness to successes and failures is part of establishing and sustaining a classroom climate and culture that is grounded in trust and compassion.

Certainly, the relationship between teachers and students develops over the course of a semester or year, and this relationship can make safe the proposition of documenting and reflecting on challenges. However, this safety deteriorates when we ask students to share their data notebooks and other self-assessment tools with peers and other adults without establishing the probability of this happening ahead of time. If other people see students' data and work in progress, the students need to be prepared for this eventuality, and they must understand why it will occur—what purpose sharing with others will hold.

It stands to reason, then, that we should definitely establish a *purpose* for sharing. We may ask students to share so they can engage in feedback conversations or so they can have support in determining next steps. These are great reasons to share mistakes and challenges, but students need to be clear about and then benefit from these decisions.

It also may be worthwhile considering limiting who will engage in data when it is still in the growth stages, in order to increase the safety students feel about taking risks that may or may not get them closer to their goals. Learning and subsequent assessment of any kind is deeply rooted in relationships, and avoiding decisions that jeopardize educational relationships requires carefully considering the implications of our decisions. Researchers Michael N. Fried and Miriam Amit (2003) explain what might happen when we involve a broader audience in data notebooks and other self-assessment tools.

> The knowledge that the students' notebooks are to be open for inspection, in particular, means that they are a public matter—they are not to be a record of students' private thoughts about what they are learning: desultory reflections; false starts; mistaken conclusions and their, perhaps embarrassing, corrections. (p. 97)

There is a big difference between reflections we keep to ourselves and reflections we choose to share with others. This difference is important in inviting students to be vulnerable and explore who they are as learners.

It all comes down to what we see as the purpose of data notebooks, portfolios, and other self-assessment tools. These processes, when done well, are intended to engage students in reflection about decisions they are making as they learn. We want students to gradually develop ownership for choices and goals, but with ownership comes investment. When students invest in their learning, the process becomes quite personal. It is reasonable to make space for students to analyze their data and set goals in relative privacy. This level of trust is quite profound and students will be grateful for it. (I have personally experienced this.)

One specific strategy to maintain student privacy is to have a designated place in data notebooks or portfolios where students can keep certain content "for their eyes only." Perhaps they can identify this section with a specific colored tab or a labeled digital folder. By allowing this slight adjustment, some work we are asking students to do might be completely independent, and other aspects may involve just the teacher and the student. Students may be comfortable sharing strategies they are trying and choices they are making with others, and this should be encouraged. However, sharing specific data, scores, and analyses may not be necessary all the time. Sharing successes with others can be very beneficial; but if we are going to share failures, we have to co-construct the conditions under which this might occur. Relationships are fragile and depend on trust. We create trust by respecting student boundaries.

Family Engagement

Now that we have reflected on the balancing act between making data notebooks, portfolios, and other self-assessment tools public or private, we can discuss the important role families play in helping students achieve success. In her article "Research for Teachers: #1 Parent Engagement," Debbie Pushor (2010), a professor in curriculum studies at the University of Saskatchewan, describes the vital role of parent engagement in student academic success. She states:

> A wealth of research concludes that students are more likely to be successful when their parents are engaged in their education. When parents are truly engaged, children:
> - attend school more regularly;
> - are better behaved;
> - have better academic outcomes;
> - have a greater sense of how to be successful in school; and
> - are more likely to graduate and go on to postsecondary education.
>
> In light of this evidence, meaningful relationships that enhance parents' opportunities to make important contributions to student learning are vital to the work of teachers.

Inviting parents and other family members to be part of students' paths to learning can have tremendous positive impacts on the very goals we are trying to achieve in education. Pushor (2010) goes on to explain:

> It is more **subtle aspects** of parent engagement that prove to be the most important—such as creating an atmosphere in the home in which education is valued, and in which high expectations and levels of support are established. When parent engagement is **linked to teaching and learning** it contributes to enhanced student results. The benefits are greater when the parent is not expected to act as another teacher. (emphasis in original)

Given this research, we need to carefully consider how we invite parents and families to be involved in students' self-assessment and goal setting. Some ways to involve families include:

- Making families aware of the decision making and goal setting students will undertake so they can support increased levels of independence and autonomy at home
- Sharing with families the steps for goal setting that you will encourage so they can reinforce these steps in other contexts
- Sharing the learning goals that will serve as the focus of self-assessment so they can follow and encourage their child's progress at home
- Inviting families into celebrations of growth and success
- Explaining why certain aspects of data notebooks and self-assessment will be private so families understand how teachers are encouraging student boundaries
- Asking for feedback and insights into student strengths to leverage these strengths in daily learning experiences
- Inviting family members to be mentors in areas of expertise that will serve student learning (for example, inviting a parent who is an author to speak with learners about their process for writing so that student goal setting can incorporate some of these skills)
- In cases where family participation is hesitant or even absent, invite students to share their efforts with a mentor or designated supportive adult; to make this need less obvious (and support social safety), you might invite all students to identify an extra support person who will interact with their documentation.

Inviting parents, family members, and support mentors into conversations about skill development and self-assessment can support a story about education that speaks to collaboration, student decision making, and a focus on strengths, prior experiences, and relationships. Learning happens within families, and this learning and support can be honored through a focus on self-assessment.

Teacher and Student Roles

This book has already explored, to some degree, the roles of both teachers and students in using data notebooks, portfolios, and other self-assessment tools. The purpose of this section is to simply review and expand on these roles, so the tools used for self-assessment move from being useful to being invaluable.

Teachers and students will always share the business of growth, but we should see a gradual shift in responsibility for decision making away from teachers and toward students as they progress through our school system. When students engage in data notebooks, portfolios, and other self-assessment tools, we want them to demonstrate as much ownership of the process as possible. Chappuis and colleagues (2012) express the importance of student decision making this way:

> Student involvement is the central shift needed in our traditional view of assessment's role in teaching and learning. The decisions that contribute the most to student learning success are made, not by adults working in the system, *but by students themselves*. *Students* decide whether the learning is worth the effort required to attain it. *Students* decide whether they are capable of reaching the learning targets. *Students* decide whether to keep learning or to quit working. It is only when students make these decisions in the affirmative that our instruction can benefit their learning. (p. 8)

We depend on students to become invested in their own learning, and building this investment and accompanying independence are key educational outcomes. Clarifying who will do what in this process can support these ends. Table 6.1 clarifies teacher and student roles in the use of data notebooks and other self-assessment tools.

TABLE 6.1: Teacher and Student Roles When Using Assessment Tools

Area of Focus	Role of the Teacher	Role of the Student
Essential (or Priority) Goals	• Clarify and map essential (or priority) standards, outcomes, or goals. These goals often emerge from mandated state or provincial documents.	• Focus on the essential (or priority) standards, outcomes, or goals in daily learning and goal setting.
Proficiency	• Develop clarity about proficiency of skill, understanding, or both (what students will do and to what degree of quality). • Share these expectations with students.	• Use exemplars, criteria, and other tools to develop understanding of proficiency. Students will use these tools during analysis.
Documentation	• Clarify, for students, which documentation (data and artifacts) they might collect and align this documentation with essential (or priority) goals. • Communicate the degree of privacy students can expect for their data notebooks and other self-assessment processes and why. • Help students determine how to organize their documentation to facilitate analysis and goal setting. • Communicate schedules and timelines for data notebooks and other self-assessment tools. • Ensure students document learning at various stages.	• Collect documentation (data and artifacts) before, during, and after learning. • Label documentation with the learning goals they represent. • Create and maintain organization of data notebooks. • Gather documentation by established deadlines.

Artifact and Data Analysis	• Select the kind of analysis that best supports the learning goals. • Explicitly teach students how to analyze data and artifacts—use predictable protocols. • Provide time for students to analyze data and artifacts and time for them to plan a response. • Model analysis so students can visualize success. • Offer suggestions for how to organize data and artifacts so they can be easily analyzed. • Nurture a classroom climate and culture that supports risk taking and mistake making.	• Engage in artifact or data analysis. • Apply protocols and processes. • Use analysis to figure out next steps. • Organize data and artifacts so analysis is easier. • Take risks, make mistakes, celebrate successes, and connect these things to decisions made.
Goal Setting	• Support students in focusing on necessary long-term goals. • Invite students to set short-term goals. • Allow students to make some decisions about steps they will take and strategies they will use. Offer ideas when appropriate. • Provide time for students to both set goals and work on those goals. • Make time for students to revisit their goals frequently and determine how they are going (strengths and needs). • Provide templates and processes to guide goal setting. • Connect goal setting to proficiency.	• Set short-term goals that align with long-term goals. • Make decisions about actions that will be taken to support goals (work alongside the teacher for options). • Use data and artifacts to guide goal setting. • Imagine future state. • Return to goals to reflect, celebrate, and make changes as needed. • Use templates and processes provided. • Use exemplars and success criteria to guide decisions. • Take ownership for decisions and consequences of those decisions.
Celebrating	• Get to know learners and discover how they like to be celebrated. • Support students in celebrating strengths and successes. • Make regular time to celebrate. • Connect celebrations to goals and decisions.	• Identify and acknowledge strengths and successes. • Determine ways to celebrate that feel good. • Celebrate with others when it makes sense. • Connect celebrations to goals and decisions.
Family Engagement	• Let families know how data notebooks and other self-assessment tools will be used. • Share successes with families when appropriate. • Engage families in supporting learning.	• Share goals, successes, and challenges of learning with family. • Accept support and encouragement. • Let teacher know of concerns.

*Visit **go.SolutionTree.com/assessment** for a free reproducible version of this table.*

It's important to remember that the level of guidance, modeling, and support you provide to students for each of these roles depends on the students' developmental age and comfort levels with the self-assessment process. For example, students in early elementary classrooms will need significant guidance when establishing the success criteria (proficiency) for specific products and performances, as well as selecting documentation, while older students can have a greater hand in co-constructing success criteria, using samples and collaborative conversations. As with any learning, ongoing observations and conversations can alert teachers to the level of support students need in developing the skills required during self-assessment.

How to Overcome Common Barriers

Despite our best efforts and the greatest of intentions, making data notebooks, portfolios, and other self-assessment tools become meaningful components of classroom learning can be difficult. Anticipating some of the barriers that make this work challenging can help us avoid trouble before it arises. The following sections detail common barriers to the effective use of self-assessment tools, namely:

- Self-assessment tools are time-consuming and interrupt learning.
- There is so much initial work that teachers lose stamina.
- The teacher does most of the work, and it takes too much time.
- Students take their failures personally, which is demotivating.
- The teacher doesn't trust students to make the right decisions.

The following sections also explain how teachers and students can avoid these pitfalls.

Self-Assessment Tools Are Time-Consuming and Interrupt Learning

This barrier can definitely happen when we start too big and are unclear about how the process of self-assessment is embedded within learning (as opposed to sitting outside it). To avoid this, we should select one or two simple tools or prompts and use them when it makes the most sense within the context of learning. Each time we plan a lesson, we might ask ourselves when it seems right to pause for a moment or two and reflect on decision making. For example, we might ask learners to quickly set a learning intention or goal at the beginning of class and then check in two-thirds of the way through to see how things are going. In another context, perhaps we have given our learners a larger formative assessment (assignment, practice quiz, review, rehearsal, or scrimmage), and it makes sense to take a little time and have students analyze their data and the artifact itself (assignment, quiz, video clip) and determine strengths and next steps.

These examples highlight the importance of this process authentically supporting learning and decision making. To ensure it does not become time consuming, assessment needs to occur when it makes the most sense, and the processes (or templates) we use need to become increasingly familiar and practical. The less text heavy and the more intuitive, the better. The actions need to be applicable immediately, and teachers must acknowledge growth, in order to build up a sense of quick wins and certainty about how these processes serve learning. We could avoid data notebooks and other self-assessment processes altogether, but we then have to acknowledge we are sustaining student dependence on teachers to make all the decisions.

There Is So Much Initial Work That Teachers Lose Stamina

There are many ideas in this book, and there are many templates and tools you could select from to facilitate self-assessment. However, make no mistake, you will have to curate which tools work best for you in your school or classroom. We can lose sight of the purpose of data notebooks, portfolios, and other self-assessment tools and spend a lot of time fixating on having students create detailed tables of contents, beautiful data spreadsheets, colorful and complicated goal sheets, and overwhelming documentation. This can get exhausting very quickly for both students and teachers, and it inevitably results in self-assessment becoming "a separate thing" as opposed to a process that serves learning.

Resist the urge to do too much, to make things too beautiful, and to require too much detail and writing (audio files work well here). Start small and build up over time so it is sustainable and doable. Remember that at the heart of self-assessment is understanding what we are trying to do, making some decisions that may or may not get us there, and finding time to reflect and make changes when needed. It is as simple as that! Pick what will support those three steps and start small.

The Teacher Does Most of the Work, and It Takes Too Much Time

The minute teachers are doing more work than students to create data notebooks, portfolios, or other self-assessment tools is when we need to stop and rethink our approaches. These tools are not for an audience, and they are not the teacher's responsibility. These tools are for students, and they must support their learning. Simple data notebooks or portfolios used to make real decisions that support real learning are far better than those with laminated and colorful pages, organized and color-coded sections, and documentation that overflows but is never analyzed or used for decision making. These are living documents, and primary responsibility for their contents has to remain with students.

Students Take Their Failures Personally, Which Is Demotivating

When any assessment process demotivates students, it is time to reflect on the purpose assessment serves and the impact it has on learners. When students perceive failure negatively, it signals a need to address the climate and culture in the classroom and the beliefs students have about themselves and their capacity to grow. Educators have work to do in communicating and reinforcing the idea that mistakes lead to understanding. There has to be a direct connection between decisions that did not lead to success and new decisions that get students closer to goals. Teachers should work with students to guide them toward choices that support success. Engaging students in data and artifacts does not guarantee the development of a growth mindset. Teachers have to help learners see how the assessment processes support growth.

As noted earlier in chapter 4 (page 71), teachers should guide students toward productive struggle as part of their path to success. Blackburn (2018) writes,

> Productive struggle means more than simply giving a student "hard work" and leaving them alone to struggle. It is a learning opportunity that requires a teacher to create, facilitate, and monitor the process, especially as students are learning how to struggle productively.

Erkens and colleagues (2017) explain that "student investment is not a guaranteed outcome of students monitoring their data. Student investment happens when teachers foster the conditions so that the assessment results are descriptive and students take action on their next steps so they grow" (p. 114). Without a climate and culture that support failure, time to respond to assessment information, and evidence of growth over time, students can certainly become discouraged. Action that leads to learning is essential.

The Teacher Doesn't Trust Students to Make the Right Decisions

At the root of self-assessment is a belief in learners and their potential to accept ownership for their own goals and decisions. If you do not believe students can become partners in education, then this process will not work. You have to believe that students can learn to engage in self-assessment, and you have to be willing to give them the time and support they need to do so. You need to see student agency as a precursor to and a product of meaningful education.

You also have to be very clear abut the purpose of self-assessment. If you are preoccupied with absolute accuracy when students are engaging in analysis, then you are situating assessment as a summative process, where accuracy is critical. If instead you remember that self-assessment is about enhancing learning, informing decision making, and celebrating interim steps, you can work to increase the accuracy of student analyses without worrying when they overestimate or underestimate their performance a little. What is most important is whether you are able to establish the next instructional moves together, with students. The premise of self-assessment is that students can be a rich part of this process.

As discussed in previous chapters, this belief is based on a *growth mindset*, as described by Dweck (2016). A growth mindset is based on people believing that their learning and intelligence can grow with time, practice, and experience. They believe that they can aquire skills and that this effort can contribute to their success. Alternatively, people with a fixed mindset believe their learning and intelligence are fixed and cannot change—success and achievement are the result of talent alone and are something one is born with or not. In order for the self-assessment process to be successful, both the teacher and student must have a growth mindset, believing that mistakes, failures, effort, and reflection lead to growth and improvement.

At the root of any expectation we hold for students is an understanding that we need to *teach*, and students can and will *learn*. This is the crux of an educational relationship. It is the job of educators to explicitly develop and consistently reinforce the skills discussed in this book. However, without belief, we have nothing.

Where to Start

Sometimes, when exploring complex concepts like self-assessment with early learners, students' right to privacy, parent engagement, and the role of teachers in self-assessment, it helps to focus on the very first steps we might take to begin. While the following five steps are not comprehensive, they are a way to begin this process if you are looking for a starting point.

1. Select a self-assessment subskill and imagine ways to develop it in early elementary students. Teach it, model it, allow student to practice, and assess it (formatively, of course). While students in elementary school and beyond can often combine several subskills at once, early elementary classrooms are places where you can focus on these skills in isolation as a way of building comfort and familiarity for students.

2. Prioritize your learning goals and build self-assessment into the instructional process. Ask early elementary students to remember, notice, and describe their decisions and then imagine different decisions.

3. Allow students time to reflect on their own goals and self-assess their own progress without showing anyone. Reassure them that they can take risks in an emotionally and socially safe context. Then stick to this decision.

4. Communicate with parents about the importance of self-assessment. Explain how it builds independence and agency. Share celebrations with parents often.

5. Take an active role in teaching students to self-assess. Model it, encourage documentation, teach students to analyze data or artifacts, and celebrate growth. Make time to develop self-assessment as its own complex skill.

QUESTIONS TO GUIDE CONVERSATION AND REFLECTION

On your own or as a part of a collaborative team, consider the following eight reflective questions.

1. How might we encourage self-assessment through emergent conversations? How might this become more intentional?
2. How consistent is self-assessment across grade levels and between subject areas? When does it seem easier, and when does it seem more challenging? How might we build consistency and agency into all classes and grade levels?
3. How often are students afforded privacy in their educational context? What does the notion of privacy in education make us think about? How do we feel about students being entitled to boundaries?
4. For whom are students self-assessing? How might we move toward intrinsic motivation?
5. How are students' families invited to share in the learning in our schools and classrooms? How authentic is this relationship?

6. What is the ratio between positive and negative communication with families? Does it vary between families? What does this tell us about equity, confidence, and values?

7. How often do teachers listen to students? How does this occur? Under what conditions? Why might it be important to increase the presence of student voice?

8. What barriers currently exist that are making self-assessment challenging? How might these barriers be mitigated?

EPILOGUE

*The big idea here is that students should take more responsibility for
their own learning, so that over time, they are able to manage their own
learning as well as, or even better, than any teacher could.*
—Dylan Wiliam

So, is self-assessment worth it? Will the creation of data notebooks, portfolios, and other self-assessment tools to support this skill yield the imagined rewards? Do the dividends justify the effort? Making self-assessment successful requires intentional planning by teachers and students, but everyone benefits when self-assessment works. In this book, I have shared some of the key components self-assessment and how using data notebooks, portfolios, and other tools can support students in developing this critical skill. Engaging in effective documentation, analysis, goal setting, and celebration ensures the process of self-assessment serves today's classrooms.

The most important thing to remember is that students' education is about more than prescribed content and skills; it is about supporting the development of thinking and feeling human beings who will become increasingly responsible for their own decisions and actions. Sandra Herbst and Anne Davies (2016) remind us:

> Engagement in learning is directly connected to students' use of cognitive, meta-cognitive, and self-regulatory strategies that monitor and guide the learning process. When students are involved in the assessment process—examining samples, co-constructing criteria, self-assessing, collecting evidence of their learning and communicating it to others—they are engaged in meaningful ways. (p. 29)

Through data notebooks, portfolios, and other self-assessment processes, we teach students how to notice the world around them, how to look at information and analyze the results of decisions made, and how to set goals that will serve them in both the short and long term. It would be difficult to argue with the importance of these skills. Deciding to embark on strengthening self-assessment as a meaningful classroom process is a decision that supports students now and in the future.

APPENDIX

Example Self-Assessment Sequence

This appendix offers an example of how you might embed self-assessment in your classroom instruction, beginning with initial goal setting and the creation of a student artifact through to revision, final reflection, and celebration. You will notice that in this example, initial instruction (on writing an extended metaphor) occurs prior to goal setting. In the initial self-assessment, the student (Sam, a tenth grader) begins by setting some short-term goals for the writing assignment and then crafts the first version of the artifact (draft).

The intention of this example is to illustrate possible self-assessment processes in which students and teachers might engage as they work through the development of a specific product. Figure A.1 (page 124) shows an overview of the learning and self-assessment sequence.

124 STUDENT SELF-ASSESSMENT

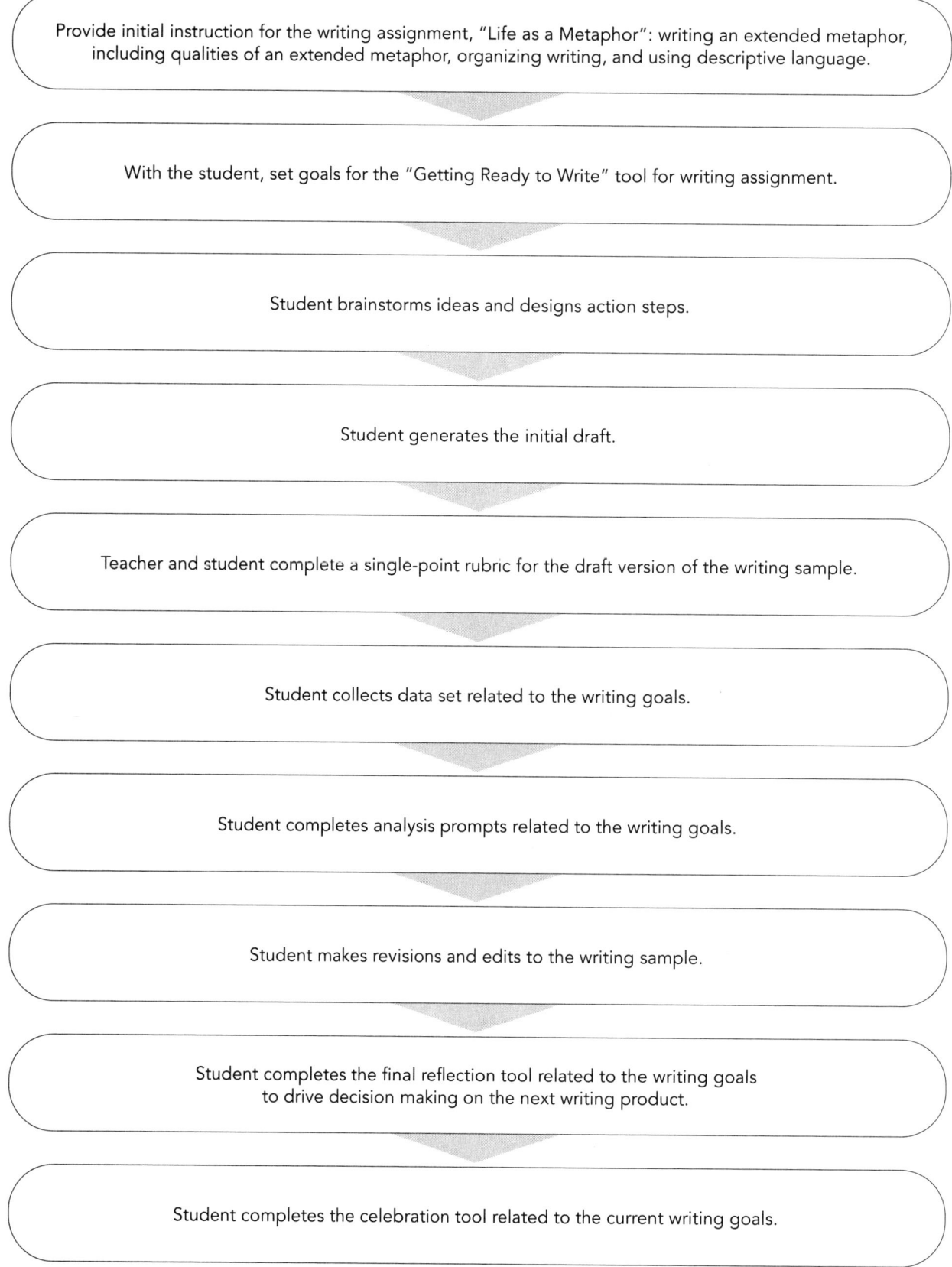

FIGURE A.1: Example learning and self-assessment sequence.

Getting Ready to Write

Name: Sam

Product: "Life as a Metaphor" writing assignment

Directions: Use the tool in figure A.2 to set goals for this assignment.

Personal Goal	Materials and Resources	Prior Knowledge and Skills	Action Steps
I am going to try to work on using more examples in my writing. I also want my organization to make sense and use better transitions.	I am going to use my writing notebook for ideas. I have been collecting ideas in there during our free writing time. I am going to make a table to make sure I have examples for my ideas. I will use the transition word list.	In my last writing assignment, I really practiced using examples but that was for making an argument. My writing usually makes sense. It is usually in good order.	Work through my metaphor. Make sure it makes sense. Try to add some examples for each part of the metaphor. Make sure I am writing things in the right order. Pay attention to transition words.

FIGURE A.2: Prepare for writing assignment.

Writing Sample: *Life Is an Elevator*

Name: Sam

In many ways, life is an elevator. First of all, halfway through you sometimes have to let people go. For example when people die in life you have to let them go. Second, sometimes you get stuck between two floors. Many times people have trouble between two stages of their lives. For example between high school and university of between university and an actual job, people don't know what to do. Thirdly, when you are at the lobby floor, all you want to do is get to the top, but once you get to the top sometimes you get sent back down. For example many people want to get to the high class, or to be rich. Once people get there, they get bored or lose their money and go back down. Last, if the elevator is stuck you can't just stay there. In life there are many stops and breakdowns but you have to get somewhere and hit the help button. Life's an elevator.

Single-Point Rubric for "Life as a Metaphor"

Name: Sam

Product: "Life as a Metaphor" writing assignment

Directions: Use the reflection tool in figure A.3 to review and reflect on your first draft. Once you have reflected, hand in your first draft and your reflection. Your teacher will follow up with feedback.

Success Criteria	Student Reflection	Proficiency	Teacher Feedback
Message	My metaphor makes sense and is something most people will know about. I used examples and sometimes more than one for an idea I had.	Metaphor is logical and relatable. Extended metaphor is well-developed with logical examples.	You chose a metaphor that is very relatable and offers many ways to connect it to a person's life. You provided examples. I wonder how you might develop a few of them a little further. I was curious about the breakdown and help button at the end. Could you expand on this a little more?
Organization	My writing makes sense. I wasn't sure whether to use more than one paragraph for this.	Logical organization leads to a clear message.	Your organization was logical. If you expand on some of your ideas a little more, you could divide your main ideas into paragraphs. This might help you really offer some rich and relatable examples that connect to readers' experiences.
Language Choices	I used the words first, second, third, and last. I feel like these words make my writing have good flow.	Transition words are varied and lead the reader through the metaphor.	You used some strong and clear transition words. You might need to expand on this as you add more details to your examples. Remember to consult your transition list for creative ways to do this.

FIGURE A.3: Single-point rubric for "Life as a Metaphor."

Data Collection: Transition Words and Use of Examples

Name: Sam

Product: "Life as a Metaphor" writing assignment

Directions: Use figure A.4 to collect data about your writing sample.

Personal Goal	Frequency	Analysis
Examples	✓ ✓ ✓	I see I didn't have an example for my last point. I could add more details to my examples. There are fewer examples than I expected.
Transition Words	✓ ✓ ✓ ✓	I used the words first, second, third, and last. I didn't really try new ones. If I do paragraphs, I'll have to add some better ones.

FIGURE A.4: Data collection for writing sample.

Analysis and Reflection

Name: Sam

Product: "Life as a Metaphor" writing assignment

Personal goals: Examples and transitions

Directions: Use your single-point rubric and data collection and analysis chart, along with figure A.5, to analyze and reflect on your writing sample.

Success Criteria	Reflection Prompts	Student Reflection	Evidence
Strengths	When it comes to the goals you set for this assignment, where do you see evidence of strength? Please share your evidence.	I think my examples are good. I think my ideas make sense. My transition words are logical.	Death and letting people go halfway Stuck between floors and stuck in a stage in life Changing directions on the elevator and changing directions in life Have to keep moving in both Transitions: first, second, third, and last
Needs	When it comes to the goals you set for this assignment, where do you see evidence of a need for more learning and practice? Please share your evidence.	My writing is just one paragraph, and I think it should be more, so I need more examples to justify using more than one paragraph. I need to expand on my examples and include more details. I need to divide my writing into paragraphs and use other transitions.	I only used one paragraph (I indented only once). Paragraphs need to be more than one sentence, so I need more examples or details in the examples I have. The transitions I mentioned above are a bit boring.

1. What commitments do you make to enhancing your assignment? *I am going to make the changes I noted in the chart (expand and paragraphs).*

2. When do you commit to have these changes completed? *Tuesday*

FIGURE A.5: Analysis and reflection chart.

Writing Sample Revision: *Life Is an Elevator*

Name: Sam

In many ways, life is an elevator. We move in different directions, always heading somewhere, and end up in new places. Ups and downs take us through our days.

Life is an elevator because halfway through you sometimes have to let people go. For example, when people die in life you have to let them go. Also, sometimes you make new friends and leave old ones. Not everyone you meet sticks around.

Another reason life is like an elevator is when sometimes you get stuck between two floors. Many times people have trouble between two stages of their lives. For example, between high school and university or between university and an actual job, people don't know what to do. Sometimes you feel stuck.

Third, when you are at the lobby floor, all you want to do is get to the top, but once you get to the top sometimes you get sent back down. For example, many people want to get to the high class, or to be rich. Once people get there, they get bored or lose their money and go back down.

Lastly, life is an elevator because if the elevator is stuck you can't just stay there. In life there are many stops and breakdowns but you have to get somewhere and hit the help button. Ellevators don't stay in one place for long and life is like that.

Life is an elevator.

Final Reflection

Name: Sam

Product: "Life as a Metaphor" writing assignment

Directions: Consider your growth and learning during this writing assignment. Use the tool in figure A.6 to engage in a final reflection on your product. Elaborate on what strategic actions you will take to approach a similar product or assignment in the future and what decisions you will make before, during, and after to ensure you are successful.

Strategic Actions *Before* Writing (Idea generation and planning)	Strategic Actions *During* Writing (Drafts and revisions)	Strategic Actions *After* Writing (Before sharing)
I will spend more time before writing to make sure I have all my examples figured out. I know I need my examples to be more detailed. I will plan to write in more than one paragraph right from the beginning. I will look at examples if they are available. This helps me know what I am supposed to do.	As I write, I will stop and check with someone else to make sure my examples are making sense. I will make sure I don't use the same transition words all the time. I will ask for ideas if I need them. I will refer to my goal sheet to remember what I am trying to do. I will also pay more attention to time so I am not rushed.	I will find someone I trust to give me good feedback to check my examples before sharing. I will also get feedback on my paragraphs to make sure they are good enough and have enough detail.

FIGURE A.6: Final reflection.

My Goals and Celebration

Directions: Use the tool in figure A.7 to determine your future goals. Then choose a learning milestone to highlight and explain how you would like to celebrate.

My writing goals:
Give good examples to make my ideas more interesting and to use transition words and phrases to make my writing flow better.
Decisions I made that got me closer to my goal:
I set goals that helped me focus on certain things. I spent time really thinking about my metaphor and making sure it was good. I fixed the things people told me needed fixing and it made my writing better.
What I would like to celebrate:
I would like to celebrate my metaphor and how much better my examples got. I think this is interesting writing for other people who have felt these things.
How I would like to celebrate:
I want to share my writing with my mom because she likes reading my ideas.

FIGURE A.7: My goals and celebrations.

REFERENCES AND RESOURCES

Action planning. (n.d.). Accessed at https://dictionary.cambridge.org/dictionary/english/action-plan on September 4, 2021.

Admiraal, W., Huisman, B., & Pilli, O. (2015). Assessment in massive open online courses. *Electronic Journal of e-Learning, 13*(4), 207–216.

Ai-Girl, T. (2004). *Exploring children's perceptions of learning*. Singapore: Marshall Cavendish Academic.

Analysis. (n.d). Accessed at www.merriam-webster.com/dictionary/analysis on August 3, 2021.

Andrade, H. L. (2019). *A critical review of research on student self-assessment*. Accessed at www.frontiersin.org/articles/10.3389/feduc.2019.00087/full on March 1, 2021.

Andrade, H. L., & Du, Y. (2007). Student responses to criteria-referenced self-assessment. *Assessment & Evaluation in Higher Education, 32*(2), 159–181.

Artifact. (n.d.). Accessed at www.merriam-webster.com/dictionary/artifact on September 2, 2021.

Bandura, A. (1977). *Social learning theory*. Englewood Cliffs, NJ: Prentice Hall.

Bateson, M. C. (1994). *Peripheral visions: Learning along the way*. New York: HarperCollins.

Baxter, P., & Norman, G. (2011). Self-assessment or self-deception? A lack of association between nursing students' self-assessment and performance. *Journal of Advanced Nursing, 67*(11), 2406–2413.

Black, P., & Wiliam, D. (1998). Inside the black box: Raising standards through classroom assessment. *Phi Delta Kappan, 80*(2), 144, 146–148.

Blackburn, B. (2018, December 18). Productive struggle is a learner's sweet spot. *Productive Struggle for All, 14*(11). Accessed at www.ascd.org/ascd-express/vol14/num11/productive-struggle-is-a-learners-sweet-spot.aspx on May 19, 2021.

Burns, E. C., Martin, A. J., & Collie, R. J. (2018). Growth goal setting in positive education: The role of personal best (PB) goal setting in promoting student well-being and academic success. In R. Stokoe (Ed.), *Global perspectives in positive education* (pp. 179–194). Melton, UK: John Catt Educational.

Centre for Imagination in Research, Culture & Education. (n.d.). *A brief guide to imaginative education*. Accessed at http://ierg.ca/about-us/a-brief-guide-to-imaginative-education on July 16, 2020.

Chappuis, J., Stiggins, R., Chappuis, S., & Arter, J. (2012). *Classroom assessment for student learning: Doing it right—using it well* (2nd ed.). Boston: Pearson.

Clandinin, D. J. & Connelly, F. M. (1995). *Teachers' professional knowledge landscapes*. New York: Teachers College Press.

Cohen, R. K., Opatsoky, D. K., Savage, J., Stevens, S. O., & Darrah, E. P. (2021). *The metacognitive student: How to teach academic, social, and emotional intelligence in every content area.* Bloomington, IN: Solution Tree Press.

Conzemius, A. E., & O'Neill, J. (2014). *The handbook for SMART school teams: Revitalizing best practices for collaboration* (2nd ed.). Bloomington, IN: Solution Tree Press.

Covey, S. R. (2020). *The 7 habits of highly effective people: Powerful lessons in personal change* (4th ed.). New York: Simon & Schuster.

Data. (n.d.). Accessed at www.merriam-webster.com/dictionary/data on September 2, 2021.

de Abreu, B. (2017). *Privacy and data in students' lives: A cultural shift in the U.S.* Accessed at http://eprints.lse.ac.uk/76259/1/Parenting%20for%20a%20Digital%20Future%20%E2%80%93%20Privacy%20and%20data%20in%20students%E2%80%99%20lives_%20a%20cultural%20shift%20in%20the%20US.pdf on July 20, 2021.

Dimich, N. (2015). *Design in five: Essential phases to create engaging assessment practice.* Bloomington, IN: Solution Tree Press.

Documentation. (n.d.). Accessed at www.merriam-webster.com/dictionary/documentation on September 2, 2021.

Doran, G. T. (1981). There's a S.M.A.R.T. way to write management's goals and objectives. *Management Review, 70*(11), 35–36.

Dueck, M. (2014). *Grading smarter, not harder: Assessment strategies that motivate kids and help them learn.* Alexandria, VA: Association for Supervision and Curriculum Development.

Dweck, C. (2016, January 13). *What having a "growth mindset" really means.* Accessed at https://hbr.org/2016/01/what-having-a-growth-mindset-actually-means on June 8, 2020.

Early Childhood Learning and Knowledge Center. (n.d.). *The importance of schedules and routines.* Accessed at https://eclkc.ohs.acf.hhs.gov/about-us/article/importance-schedules-routines on July 15, 2021.

Erkens, C. (2013, October 21). *Data notebooks* [Blog post]. Retrieved from www.anamcaraconsulting.com/wordpress/2013/10/21/data-notebooks on April 6, 2020.

Erkens, C., Schimmer, T., & Dimich, N. (2017). *Essential assessment: Six tenets for bringing hope, efficacy, and achievement to the classroom.* Bloomington, IN: Solution Tree Press.

Erkens, C., Schimmer, T., & Dimich, N. (2019). *Growing tomorrow's citizens in today's classrooms: Assessing 7 critical competencies.* Bloomington, IN: Solution Tree Press.

Fried, M. N., & Amit, M. (2003). Some reflections on mathematics classroom notebooks and their relationship to the public and private nature of student practices. *Educational Studies in Mathematics, 53*(2), 91–112.

Goal setting. (n.d.). Accessed at https://dictionary.cambridge.org/dictionary/english/goal-setting on September 4, 2021.

Greene, M. (2000). *Releasing the imagination: Essays on education, the arts, and social change.* San Francisco: Jossey-Bass.

Gregory, K., Cameron, C., & Davies, A. (2011). *Self-assessment and goal setting* (2nd ed.). Bloomington, IN: Solution Tree Press.

Hall, P., & Simeral, A. (2015). *Teach, reflect, learn: Building your capacity for success in the classroom.* Alexandria, VA: Association for Supervision and Curriculum Development.

Hattie, J. A. C. (2012). *Visible learning for teachers: Maximizing impact on learning.* London: Routledge.

Hattie, J. A. C., & Donoghue, G. M. (2016). *Learning strategies: A synthesis and conceptual model.* Accessed at www.nature.com/articles/npjscilearn201613 on March 24, 2021.

Hattie, J. A. C., & Timperley, H. (2007). The power of feedback. *Review of Educational Research, 77*(1), 81–112.

Herbst, S., & Davies, A. (2016). *Grading, reporting, and professional judgment in elementary classrooms.* Courtenay, Canada: Connect2Learning.

Jarry, J. (2020). *The Dunning-Kruger effect is probably not real.* Accessed at www.mcgill.ca/oss/article/critical-thinking/dunning-kruger-effect-probably-not-real on July 22, 2021.

Jensen, E. (2019). *Poor students, rich teaching: Seven high-impact mindsets for students from poverty* (Rev. ed.). Bloomington, IN: Solution Tree Press.

Kruger, J., & Dunning, D. (1999). Unskilled and unaware of it: How difficulties in recognizing one's own incompetence lead to inflated self-assessments. *Journal of Personality and Social Psychology, 77*(6), 1121–1134.

Leffler, B., & Crauder, B. (2011). T'was the start of science notebooking: A poem to celebrate a vital classroom tool. *Science and Children, 49*(3), 56–61.

McLeod, S. (2016). *Albert Bandura's social learning theory.* Accessed at www.simplypsychology.org/bandura.html on June 1, 2020.

McTighe, J., & Wiggins, G. (2013). *Essential questions: Opening doors to student understanding.* Alexandria, VA: Association for Supervision and Curriculum Development.

Metacognition. (n.d.). Accessed at www.merriam-webster.com/dictionary/metacognition on September 2, 2021.

Meyer, B., & Latham, N. (2008). *Implementing electronic portfolios: Benefits, challenges, and suggestions.* Accessed at https://er.educause.edu/articles/2008/2/implementing-electronic-portfolios-benefits-challenges-and-suggestions on July 14, 2021.

Nordengren, C. (2019). *Goal-setting practices that support a learning culture.* Accessed at https://kappanonline.org/goal-setting-practices-support-learning-culture-nordengren on July 18, 2021.

Organisation for Economic Co-operation and Development. (2017). *The OECD handbook for innovative learning environments.* Accessed at https://read.oecd-ilibrary.org/education/the-oecd-handbook-for-innovative-learning-environments_9789264277274-en#page1 on July 16, 2021.

Orsmond, P., Merry, S., & Reiling, K. (2002). The use of exemplars and formative feedback when using student derived marking criteria in peer and self-assessment. *Assessment & Evaluation in Higher Education, 27*(4), 309–323.

Porosoff, L., & Weinstein, J. (2018). *Empower your students: Tools to inspire a meaningful school experience, grades 6–12.* Bloomington, IN: Solution Tree Press.

Pushor, D. (2010). *Research for teachers: #1 parent engagement.* Accessed at www.etfo.ca/SupportingMembers/Resources/R4Tdocs/Research%20for%20Teachers%20-%20Number%201%20-%20Parent%20Engagement.pdf on August 18, 2021.

Qualitative. (n.d.). Accessed at www.merriam-webster.com/dictionary/qualitative on September 2, 2021.

Quantitative. (n.d.). Accessed at www.merriam-webster.com/dictionary/quantitative on September 2, 2021.

Reflection. (n.d.). Accessed at www.merriam-webster.com/dictionary/reflection on August 3, 2021.

Ross, J. A. (2006). The reliability, validity, and utility of self-assessment. *Practical Assessment, Research, and Evaluation, 11*(10), 1–13.

Sanchez, C. E., Atkinson, K. M., Koenka, A. C., Moshontz, H., & Cooper, H. (2017). Self-grading and peer-grading for formative and summative assessments in 3rd through 12th grade classrooms: A meta-analysis. *Journal of Educational Psychology, 109*(8), 1049–1066.

Schimmer, T. (2014). *Ten things that matter from assessment to grading.* Boston: Pearson.

Seitz, H. (2008). The power of documentation in the early childhood classroom. *Young Children.* Accessed at www.naeyc.org/sites/default/files/globally-shared/downloads/PDFs/resources/pubs/seitz.pdf on July 18, 2021.

Self-evalutation. (n.d.). Accessed at www.merriam-webster.com/dictionary/self-evaluation on September 2, 2021.

Self-regulation. (n.d.). Accessed at www.merriam-webster.com/dictionary/self-regulation on September 2, 2021.

Self-testing. (n.d.). Accessed at www.merriam-webster.com/dictionary/self-testing on September 2, 2021.

Souers, K. V. M., & Hall, P. (2019). *Relationship, responsibility, and regulation: Trauma-invested practices for fostering resilient learners.* Alexandria, VA: Association for Supervision and Curriculum Development.

Souers, K., & Hall, P. (2016). *Fostering resilient learners: Strategies for creating a trauma-sensitive classroom.* Alexandria, VA: Association for Supervision and Curriculum Development.

Spiller, D. (2012). *Assessment matters: Self-assessment and peer assessment.* Hamilton, New Zealand: University of Waikato.

Stronge, J. H., & Grant, L. W. (2014). *Student achievement goal setting: Using data to improve teaching and learning.* New York: Taylor & Francis.

Thompson, M., & Wiliam, D. (2007, April). *Tight but loose: A conceptual framework for scaling up school reforms* [Conference presentation]. Educational Research Association Conference, Chicago, IL.

Tomlinson, C. A. (2005). Grading and differentiation: Paradox or good practice? *Theory Into Practice, 44*(3), 262–269.

Usher, A., & Kober, N. (2012). *Student motivation: An overlooked piece of school reform.* Washington, DC: Center for Education Policy.

Wagner, D. (2017). *4 tools to help kids develop empathy and cultural humility.* Accessed at www.kqed.org/mindshift/49609/4-tools-to-help-kids-develop-empathy-and-cultural-humility on June 8, 2020.

White, K. (2016, February 22). *Developing the sub-habits of self-assessment* [Blog post]. Accessed at https://allthingsassessment.info/2016/02/22/developing-the-sub-habits-of-self-assessment on March 24, 2021.

White, K. (2017). *Softening the edges: Assessment practices that honor K–12 teachers and learners.* Bloomington, IN: Solution Tree Press.

White, K. (2019). *Unlocked: Assessment as the key to everyday creativity in the classroom.* Bloomington, IN: Solution Tree Press.

Wierda, B. (2015, August 13). *Using student data as a tool in self-directed learning* [Blog post]. Accessed at www.leaderinme.org/blog/using-student-data April 25, 2021.

Wiggins, G., & McTighe, J. (2005). *Understanding by design* (Expanded 2nd ed.). Alexandria, VA: Association for Supervision and Curriculum Development.

Wiliam, D. (2018). *Embedded formative assessment* (2nd ed.). Bloomington, IN: Solution Tree Press.

INDEX

A

academic growth, 14
accessibility, of documentation, 23
achievement, connecting with goals, 77–78
action planning
    definition of, 22
    documentatin as catalyst for, 28–29
    tools for, 61, 67
agency
    in decision making, 10
    goal setting and, 72, 75
Ai-Girl, T., 11
alignment, 30, 100
Amit, M., 112
analysis, 10, 45–69, 115
    activities in, 47
    data, 55–57, 58
    definition of, 22, 46
    engagement in, 47
    feedback and, 48–49
    invitation into, 16
    modeling, 50
    process, 53–54
    prompts for, 55, 57–58, 59
    and reflection chart, 129
    of relationships between two artifacts, 54–55
    scenario on, 45–46
    of single artifacts, 50–51
    skills for, 46–47
    strategies and processes related to, 51, 53–54
    two-column approach to, 60
    what it looks like, 49
Andrade, H. L., 9, 10, 11
Arter, J., 7
artifacts, 115
    analysis of relationship between two, 54–55
    analysis of single artifact, 50–51
    comparing multiple, 55, 56
    decision making and reflection on, 50–51
    definition of, 22
    examining for strengths first, 102
    reflecting students at moments in time, 20
    types of, 21
assessment. *See also* self-assessment
    as catalyst for learning, 10–11
    preparation for, 10
    as state of impermanence, 14–15
attention, 4
autonomy, 11
    data notebooks, portfolios, and, 20
    in goal setting, 78–79

B

Bateson, M. C., 45
Blackburn, B., 74
brainstorming, 28, 47, 55, 81

C

celebrations, 16, 97–107
    benefits of, 98–99

engagement with data and, 57–58
goals and, 80
grounds for, 99–100
meaningful, 100–101
modeling, 102
scenario on, 97–98
student and teacher roles in, 115
tools for, 102, 104–107
where to start with, 101–102
Centre for Imagination in Research, Culture, and Education, 73
challenge, supporting the right amount of, 13–14
Chappuis, J., 7, 114
Chappuis, S., 7
check ins, 76, 77
Clandinin, D. J., 21
clarity, 29–30
co-construction, 48
Cohen, R. K., 79
collaboration, 11–14
in goal setting, 79
student identities/worldviews and, 13
supporting the right amount of challenge, 13–14
commitment
celebration and, 99
collaboration and, 12
to goals, 79
competencies, reflecting on, 81, 84
compliance, 12
confidence, 20–21
false, 58
confidentiality, 29
Connelly, F. M., 21
consequences, allowing students to experience, 14–15
context, 55
cooperative play, 100
Covey, S. R., 71
Crauder, B., 47
creative play, 2
Culkin, J. M., 9
cultural humility, 13

culture
collaboration reflecting diversity in, 13
safe classroom, 21
curation, 20
of focus, 21–23
by students, 28

D

Darrah, E. P., 79
data
analysis of, 55–57, 58, 115
collection of, 128
definition of, 22
documenting in various ways, 58–60
data notebooks, 5–6, 15–16
accessible, 23
curation of, 20
prerequisites for setting up, 29–30
privacy with, 113
promoting growth and learning with, 31–33
qualities of documentation for, 27–29
setup recommendations for, 30–31
data sets, 5
connection between multiple, 59–60
sample, 58, 59
Davies, A., 121
de Abreu, B., 112
decision making, 1, 10
agency in, 10
analysis of artifacts and, 50–51
celebrations and, 99
daily, 77, 91, 93
evidence-based, 28
importance of, 114
individual/group needs and, 22–23
inspirational tools with, 74–75
investment and ownership in, 5, 11–13
shared ownership in, 48
skills, 25, 26–27
trust and, 117–118
Design in Five: Essential Phases to Create Engaging Assessment Practice (Dimich), 12, 110

developmental appropriateness, 28, 100
    early elementary self-assessment, 109–111
    goal setting and, 79
Dimich, N., 12, 15, 17, 47, 97, 117
    on goals, 110
    on goal setting, 76
diversity, collaboration reflecting, 13
documentation, 5–6, 16. *See also* data notebooks; portfolios
    accessible, 23
    annotation of, 60, 62
    considerations for analysis of, 48–49
    of data, 58–60
    definition of, 22
    formative *vs.* summative, 31
    labeling, 30
    learning from, 19–20
    of less-proficient work, 20
    organizational structure of, 23–24
    selection of, 27–29
    skills for analyzing, 46–47
    subskills of self-assessment, 24–27
    time limits for, 30
    tools to support, 34–35, 36–44
    where to start with, 34
Donoghue, G. M., 77
Du, Y., 10
Dueck, M., 11
Dweck, C., 14, 117–118

E

Early Childhood Learning and Knowledge Center, 24
efficacy, 10, 11
    definition of, 15
    goal setting and, 72
effort, 4–5
empathizing, forgiving skills, 25, 26
engagement, 121
    with data, 57–58
    in data/artifact analysis, 47
    family, 113, 115
    in goal setting, 75–76

English language arts, 81, 87
English learners (ELs), 23
Erkens, C., 12, 15, 16, 17, 97, 117
essential questions, 77
evidence, 4
    curation of focus and, 23
    documenting, 5, 28
exemplars, 74
experience, learning from, 19–20

F

failure, 117
false confidence, 58
family engagement, 113, 115
feedback, 21, 30
    on celebrations, 101
    exemplars and, 74
    from family, 113
    reflection on, 31
    types of, 48–49
focus, 4
    curated, 21–23
    early elementary, 110
Fried, M. N., 112
future state, 4, 72–73, 81

G

goal setting, 31–33, 71–96
    achievement and, 77–78
    check ins, 76, 77
    considerations for, 75–79
    daily, 82, 91
    definition of, 22
    developmental appropriateness in, 100
    elements of, 73–75
    example of, 131
    during exploration, 82, 90
    hope, resilience, and, 74
    imagination in, 73
    inspirational tools for, 74–75
    monitoring, 82, 96

routines for, 80–81
scenario on, 71–72
short- and long-term, 77–78, 81, 85–86, 88–89
student and teacher roles in, 115
timing of, 75–76
tools to support, 81–96
where to start with, 81
goals
action for setting, 16
celebrations and, 99–100
characteristics of strong, 78
individual, 31
monitoring, 31
ownership of, 78–79
role of in education, 73
tools for identifying, 39
values and, 101
grades and grading, 21
Grant, L., 77
Greene M., 73
group reflections, 2
growth
celebrating, 97–107
documentation showing, 28
promoting with data notebooks and portfolios, 31–33
tracking, 61, 65
growth mindset, 14–15, 117–118

H
Hall, P., 15, 19
Hattie, J., 12–13
Hattie, J. A. C., 48, 77
Herbst, S., 121
hope, 74, 75

I
identities, 13
Ildan, M. M., 109
imagination, 73
goal setting and, 75

independence, 10, 11, 99–100
goal setting and, 75
instruction
for creating data displays, 30
goal setting and, 77
investment, 5, 117
definition of, 12
qualities of, 12–13

J
Jensen, E., 74

K
Knowing What Counts: Self-Assessment and Goal Setting (Andrade), 11
Kober, N., 77

L
Latham, N., 15
learning
assessment as a catalyst for, 10–11
productive struggle and, 74
promoting with data notebooks and portfolios, 31–33
from reflection, 19–20
shared language for, 21, 22
sustaining, 99
learning environments, 13, 24, 29, 79
learning goals, 9
alignment with, 30
documentation and, 27–28
forward momentum and, 27–28
relationship between two artifacts and, 54–55
setting, 76
sharing with students, 21
student understanding of, 29–30
targets within, 57
Leffler, B., 47

M
margin symbols, 60, 62

marginalization, 13
McTighe, J., 77
meaning
    celebrations and, 100–101
    goal setting and, 80
mentor texts, 75
Merry, S., 74
metacognition, 79, 121
    definition of, 22
metacognitive experience, 14
metacognitive knowledge, 14
metacognitive skills, 14
The Metacognitive Student (Cohen, Opatosky, Savage, Stevens, & Darrah), 79
meta-learning skills, 11
Meyer, B., 15
mindset, 14–15
    growth, 117–118
modeling, 102
    analysis, 50
motivation, 16, 117

N

Nordengren, C., 76, 77
noticing, remembering, describing skills, 25, 26, 110

O

Opatosky, D. K., 79
optimism, 1
    growth mindset and, 14–15
Organisation for Economic Co-operation and Development (OECD), 13, 29
organizing, revising, revisiting skills, 25, 27
Orsmond, P., 74
ownership, 5
    of goals, 78–79

P

personalization, 29
personal-level feedback, 48
photography, 23
Poor Students, Rich Teaching (Jensen), 74

Porosoff, L., 100–101
portfolios, 5–6, 15–16
    accessible, 23
    curation of, 20
    prerequisites for setting up, 29–30
    privacy with, 113
    promoting growth and learning with, 31–33
    setup recommendations for, 30–31
"The Power of Documentation in the Early Childhood Classroom" (Seitz), 75
"The Power of Feedback" (Hattie & Timperley), 48
praise, 14, 31
predictability, 20–21
    of supports, 24
predicting, visualizing, imagining skills, 25, 26
preferences, identifying student, 34–35, 38, 101
priorities, 21–23
    on analysis, 50
privacy, 111–112
problem solving, 75
process analysis, 53–54
process-level feedback, 48–49
productive struggle, 74
"Productive Struggle Is a Learner's Sweet Spot" (Blackburn), 74
proficiency, 114
progress tracking, 60–61, 64
    in assessments, 82, 95
purpose, 20
    documentation organizational structure and, 23–24
Pushor, D., 113

Q

qualitative, definition of, 22
quantitative, definition of, 22
quick wins, 20, 80, 116

R

reading skills, 61, 68
reflection, 1, 131
    on celebrating growth, 102–103
    on competencies, 81, 84

definition of, 22, 46
documentation as catalyst for, 28–29
early elementary level, 111
on goal setting, 82–83
goal setting and, 82, 92
group, 2
inviting, 5
learning from, 19–20
modeling, 102
on reading skills, 61, 68
on strategies and processes related to artifacts and data, 51, 53–54
of student identities and worldviews, 13
tools for, 34–35, 36–37
on work samples, 60, 63
Reiling, K., 74
relating, comparing, analyzing, connecting skills, 25, 26
relationships
    data notebooks, portfolios, and, 20
    goal setting and, 72
    student-teacher, 11–12, 112
    between two artifacts, analyzing, 54–55
"Research for Teachers: #1 Parent Engagement" (Pushor), 113
resilience, 74
Ross, J. A., 10
routines, 24
    in goal setting, 80–81

S

safe classroom culture, 21, 29
safety issues, 111–112
samples, 74–75
Savage, J., 79
scheduling, 30
Schimmer, T., 11, 12, 15, 17, 97, 117
Seitz, H., 75
selected-response questions, 58
self-assessment
    academic growth and, 13–14
    checklist for tracking, 100, 104
    collaborative effort in, 11–14

    common attributes of, 4–5
    considerations for, 20–24
    data notebooks and portfolios for, 5–6
    definition of, 9, 22
    early elementary, 109–111
    effective, 9–10
    embracing, 1–7
    examples of, 2–5
    frequency of, 1
    importance of, 1, 7, 9
    instruction in, 10
    making a case for, 9–18
    overcoming barriers in, 116–118
    paradigm shifts for, 10–15
    prerequisites for setting up, 29–30
    reflection on, 17–18
    research on, 9
    sequence for, 123–132
    setting up for, 19–24, 29–31
    subskills of, 24–27, 110
    teacher and student roles in, 113–116
    tools for, 16–17
    value of, 121
    where to start, 17
self-evaluation, 46
    definition of, 22
SELf-questions, 79
self-regulation, 25, 26–27, 121
    definition of, 22
    feedback on, 49
self-testing, definition of, 22
Simeral, A., 15, 19
single-point rubric, 60, 63, 127
SMART goals, 75, 78
social skills, 31
Softening the Edges: Assessment Practices that Honor K–12 Teachers and Learners (White), 80
Stevens, S. O., 79
Stiggins, R., 7
strategies
    analysis of success of, 55
    observable and in-the-head, 60

Stronge, J., 77
student roles, 113–116
success criteria, 55
    reflecting on, 61, 66
    student understanding of, 29–30
    timing for establishing, 76
support, 5
    predictable, 24

T

task-level feedback, 48
teacher roles, 113–116
templates
    to compare multiple artifacts, 55, 56
    for data/artifact analysis, 58
    sample process analysis, 53–54
    for single artifact analysis, 51, 52
Thompson, M., 48
time, 5
    estimating, for student self-assessment, 29
    for goal setting, 72–73, 75–76
    learning goals and, 9
    for self-assessment, 116, 117
Timperley, H., 48
Tomlinson, C. A., 99
transparency, 29–30
trust, 112, 117–118
two-column analysis approach, 60

U

understanding by design (UbD), 77
Unlocked: Assessment as the Key to Everyday Creativity in the Classroom (White), 11, 76
Usher, A., 77

V

values, 100–101
videos, 23
Visible Learning for Teachers (Hattie), 12–13

W

Wagner, D., 13
Weinstein, J., 100–101
"What Having a 'Growth Mindset' Actually Means" (Dweck), 14
White, K., 11
Wierda, B., 31
Wiggins, G., 77
Wiliam D., 14, 20–21, 48, 121
work habits, 31
worldviews, 13
writing
    preparation for, 125
    revision of, 130

Softening the Edges
Katie White

The assessment process can be a rich experience for you and your students. With *Softening the Edges*, you'll discover how to design, deliver, and differentiate instruction and assessment to address learners' diverse intellectual and emotional needs. By creating an effective assessment architecture, you can ensure your students are invested in their own learning and have the confidence to face any learning challenge.
BKF781

Unlocked
Katie White

Creativity enhances the quality of our lives, encouraging us to look deeper, search wider, and explore multiple perspectives. With *Unlocked* by Katie White, you'll discover how to effectively connect creativity and assessment within any classroom setting. A variety of practical ideas and tools helps you design rich, authentic learning experiences that encourage inquiry and creative development rather than compliance and "right" answers.
BKF851

Essential Assessment
Cassandra Erkens, Tom Schimmer, and Nicole Dimich Vagle

Discover how to use the power of assessment to instill hope, efficacy, and achievement in your students. With this research-based resource, you'll explore six essential tenets of assessment—assessment purpose, communication of assessment results, accurate interpretation, assessment architecture, instructional agility, and student investment—that will help deepen your understanding of assessment to not only meet standards but also enhance students' academic success and self-fulfillment.
BKF752

Instructional Agility
Cassandra Erkens, Tom Schimmer, and Nicole Dimich Vagle

The true power of assessment comes when emerging results determine what comes next in student learning. This practical resource empowers readers to become instructionally agile—moving seamlessly among instruction, formative assessment, and feedback—to enhance student engagement, proficiency, and ownership of learning. Each chapter concludes with reflection questions that assist readers in determining next steps for supporting the whole child and the whole learning process.
BKF764

You Can Learn!
Tim Brown and William M. Ferriter

Great learning starts when students believe in their academic abilities. In *You Can Learn!*, authors Tim Brown and William M. Ferriter introduce intentional and purposeful steps collaborative teams can take to increase the self-efficacy of every learner. By incorporating the book's research-backed practices, your PLC will cultivate a culture where students at every grade level see themselves as competent learners fully capable of succeeding in school and beyond.
BKG020

Visit SolutionTree.com or call 800.733.6786 to order.

"Excellent engagement in what truly matters in **assessment**.

Great examples!"

—Carol Johnson, superintendent,
Central Dauphin School District, Pennsylvania

PD Services

Our experts draw from decades of research and their own experiences to bring you practical strategies for designing and implementing quality assessments. You can choose from a range of customizable services, from a one-day overview to a multiyear process.

Book your assessment PD today!
888.763.9045

Solution Tree